THE LITTLE BOOK OF JUDAS

Brendan Kennelly was born in 1936 in Ballylongford, Co. Kerry; and was educated at St Ita's College, Tarbert, Co. Kerry, and at Trinity College, Dublin, where he has been Professor of Modern Literature since 1973. He has published more than twenty books of poems, including six volumes of selected poems, most recently *A Time for Voices: Selected Poems 1960-1990* (Bloodaxe, 1990) and *Breathing Spaces: Early Poems* (Bloodaxe, 1992). His latest books are *The Man Made of Rain* (Bloodaxe, 1998), written after he survived major heart surgery (available in hardback and paperback editions as well as on a double-cassette tape), and two new collections, *Begin* (Bloodaxe, 1999) and *Glimpses* (Bloodaxe, 2001).

He is best-known for two controversial poetry books, *Cromwell*, published in Ireland in 1983 and in Britain by Bloodaxe in 1987, and his epic poem *The Book of Judas*, (Bloodaxe, 1991), which topped the Irish bestsellers list: a shorter version was published by Bloodaxe in 2002 as *The Little Book of Judas*. His third epic, *Poetry My Arse* (Bloodaxe, 1995), did much to outdo these in notoriety.

His translations of Irish poetry are available in *Love of Ireland: Poems from the Irish* (Mercier Press, 1989). He has edited several anthologies, including *The Penguin Book of Irish Verse* (1970; 2nd edition 1981), *Between Innocence and Peace: Favourite Poems of Ireland* (Mercier Press, 1993), *Ireland's Women: Writings Past and Present*, with Katie Donovan and A. Norman Jeffares (Gill & Macmillan, 1994), and *Dublines*, with Katie Donovan (Bloodaxe Books, 1995). He has published two novels, *The Crooked Cross* (1963) and *The Florentines* (1967).

He is also a celebrated dramatist whose plays include versions of *Antigone* (Peacock Theatre, Dublin, 1986; Bloodaxe, 1996); *Medea*, premièred in the Dublin Theatre Festival in 1988, toured in England in 1989 by the Medea Theatre Company, and broadcast by BBC Radio 3 and published by Bloodaxe in 1991; *The Trojan Women* (Peacock Theatre & Bloodaxe, 1993); and Lorca's *Blood Wedding* (Northern Stage, Newcastle & Bloodaxe, 1996).

His *Journey into Joy: Selected Prose*, edited by Åke Persson, was published by Bloodaxe in 1994, along with *Dark Fathers into Light*, a critical anthology on his work edited by Richard Pine. Åke Persson has also published *That Fellow with the Fabulous Smile: A Tribute to Brendan Kennelly* (Bloodaxe, 1996).

His cassette recordings include *The Man Made of Rain* (Bloodaxe, 1998) and *The Poetry Quartets: 4*, shared with Paul Durcan, Michael Longley and Medbh McGuckian (The British Council / Bloodaxe Books, 1999).

THE LITTLE BOOK OF
JUDAS

BRENDAN KENNELLY

BLOODAXE BOOKS

ISBN: 1 85224 584 0

First published 2002 by
Bloodaxe Books Ltd,
Highgreen,
Tarset,
Northumberland NE48 1RP.

The original edition of *The Book of Judas* was first
published by Bloodaxe Books in three editions in 1991
(1 85224 170 5 / 171 3 / 172 1) and reprinted in 1992.

www.bloodaxebooks.com
For further information about Bloodaxe titles
please visit our website or write to
the above address for a catalogue.

Bloodaxe Books Ltd acknowledges
the financial assistance of Northern Arts.

Cover printing by J. Thomson Colour Printers Ltd, Glasgow.

Printed in Great Britain by
Cromwell Press Ltd, Trowbridge, Wiltshire.

For all good dreams
      twisted, exploited and betrayed.
For all those
      conveniently and mindlessly damned
            by you and me.
And for all those writing and unwriting
            poets of humanity
                  who have a bash
                        at comprehending the incomprehensible.

THE LITTLE BOOK OF JUDAS

from The Book of Judas: a poem

PREFACE

The imagination provides the most effective means of confronting and expressing the prejudices and inherited hatreds buried in the self until they exist before our eyes like so many lucid accusations confirming Ibsen's belief that poetry is a court of judgment on the soul. But it's more, much more than that. In a long poem, *Cromwell*, I tried to open my mind, heart and imagination to the full, fascinating complexity of a man I was from childhood taught, quite simply, to hate. A learned hate is hard to unlearn. It would be easy enough to go through life hoarding and nourishing such hate, feeding it dutifully with endless "proofs", thus keeping alive the explosive frenzies that fuel political situations such as that in Northern Ireland. But when one tries to substitute the uncertainties of altruistic exploration for the certainties of inherited hate, one is immediately disrupting and challenging one's "cultural legacy", spitting in the faces of the authoritative fathers and their revered, unimpeachable wisdom. The process of unlearning hate is a genuine insult to some, particularly those whose prejudices are called convictions.

There is something in Irish life which demands that you over-simplify practically everything. This is another way of saying that everybody must be labelled, made readily accessible, explainable. Protestant, Catholic, Dub, Northerner, Culchie, etc, are such labels. Stick any of these labels on a man or a woman, a boy or a girl, and you needn't bother yourself with further enquiry into their characters or minds. The problems of complex personality are easily solved. The label tells you all you need to know. Kerryman, Jewboy, Proddie Dog, Southsider, Northsider. 'Ah, sure, the bowsie never read a book in his life!' *Label*. Judas. Now, we know. We have him in his place. The rest is as clear as daylight. We know him to the core. Anachronistic ass. Boisterous bollocks.

But there is an electricity in the air that burns the labels and restores the spirit of investigative uncertainty. Poetry tries to plug in to this electricity, to let it thrill and animate one's ways of feeling and thinking and seeing. This electricity is what the labels fear. This electricity makes room for all the voices of the damned and outcast, the horrible archetypes for whom, in the opinion of many "decent people", there is no ear, no hope of redemption; and because no hope is allowed, these "horrible souls" can be blamed for practically anything. Recently, an English football manager was screamingly headlined JUDAS in an English paper because he changed his mind or 'went back on his word'. Judas was in no position to write a protesting letter to that newspaper. If he had, would the editor have published it? And in what spirit?

How must men and women who cannot write back, who must absorb the full thump of accusation without hope of reply, who have no voices because we know they're "beyond all hope", feel in their cold, condemned silence? In *The Book of Judas* I wished to create the voice of a condemned man writing back to me, trained and educated to condemn him. How shall I listen to someone who, I am told, has no right to a voice? If I could stretch myself to let the butcher Cromwell speak for himself, articulate his position across centuries of mechanical, hate-filled condemnation, and in the process discover that he had a lot of things to point out to me, to my shame and illumination, might I not also learn to let the outcast scapegoat Judas, suddenly electrified with protean virtuosity, yet remaining dubious, speak back and out from his icy black corner of history, or my pathetic little mind scraping at that black ice? The moment I surrendered to the voice from that icy black corner, the electricity began to flow, the questions erupted, the answers ran away to hide in some cosy little corner of their own. We all learn the nature of the possibilities of our own particular little corner.

The damned soul has a special perspective on us all, but how can we believe him, how can we believe one who is a liar and traitor by instinct? Above all, how can this be poetry? The questions kept coming as I wrote and re-wrote the poem over eight years. Was Judas a fall guy in some sublime design he didn't even begin to understand? What was he trying to prove? Was he a not-so-bright or a too-bright politician? A man whose vision of things was being throttled by another, more popular vision? A loner in an organised bunch? One who knew the dynamising power of a timely moment of betrayal? Simply an envious bastard? One who knew how to shock others into a new awareness of their situation? A man wanting to test the limits of his own intelligent, speculative, vicious potential? A spirit not confined to the man who bore the name Judas but one more alive and consequential now at the famined, bloated, trivialised, analytical, bomb-menaced, progressive, money-mad, reasonable beginning of the twenty-first century than ever before? Is Judas by definition the most contemporary of contemporaries? The Judasvoice is odd and ordinary, freakish and free, severed and pertinent, twisting what it glimpses of reality into parodies of what is taken for granted, convinced (if it's convinced of anything) that we live in an age almost helplessly devoted to ugliness, that the poisoned world we have created is simply *what we are*, and cannot be justified or explained away by science or industry or money or education or progress. To this extent, Judas knows nothing is external: where we are is who we are, what we create is merely the symmetry of our dreams. It is therefore insane to blame anybody but ourselves. But can we believe Judas? Or what he calls his poetry? How can the damned man be, even for a moment, admitted into our hearts and minds? Should he be? Why? Does he not deserve not to be heard? Not a single, bloody, crucifying word?

The Gaelic novelist Máirtín Ó Cadhain once said to me that in Ireland we divert attention from serious issues by creating a hubbub about trivial matters. I never cease to be amazed and amused at the power of triviality over serious minds. (I include myself, insofar as I can claim to be serious-minded.) In this poem I wanted to capture the relentless, pitiless anecdotalism of Irish life, the air swarming with nutty little sexual parables, the platitudinous bonhomie sustained by venomous undercurrents, the casual ferocious gossip, the local industry of rumour-making and spreading, always remembering that life is being parodied, that this Christian culture itself is a parody of what may once have been a passion. There's an atrocious tendency in Irish life, especially in Dublin, to dismiss people by turning them into sad or clownish parodies of themselves. I believe that the culture of these islands, is, broadly speaking, Christian. I have no wish to offend non-Christians, I'm merely stating a belief. I also believe that this culture is now in an advanced state of self-parody. Or, if you wish, in an advanced state of self-betrayal, playing Judas to itself. In this poem I wanted this man to talk to himself, this culture to mutter to itself of what is lost or forgotten or betrayed or grotesquely twisted in memory. And appallingly obvious now. Yet there are no answers. And what questions must be asked?

I wonder if many people feel as I do – that in the society we have created it is very difficult to give your full, sustained attention to anything or anybody for long, that we are compelled to half-do a lot of things, to half-live our lives, half-dream our dreams, half-love our loves? We have made ourselves into half-people. Half-heartedness is a slow, banal killer. It is also, paradoxically, a creepy pathway towards "success", especially if the half-heartedness is of the polished variety. I think it was D.H. Lawrence who said that the real tragedy of modern man is the loss of heart. I don't think so. I believe our tragedy is the viability of our half-heartedness, our insured, mortgaged, welfare voyage of non-discovery, the committed, corrosive involvement with forces, created by ourselves, that ensure our lives will be half-lived. There's a sad refusal here. A rejection of the unique, fragile gift.

Have we refused some love-offering we should have accepted? Have we organised and unionised ourselves into semi-paralytics? Is Judas a shrewd refuser of what might have made him loveable and vulnerable rather than – whatever he is? How much of our law of success is bound up with knowing what and how to refuse? Is this refusal-betrayal necessary if one is to be numbered among "decent people"? How "respectable" is Judas? To what extent have we elected Judas to be our real redeemer from the consequences of what we have ourselves created but like to blame somebody else for, when "things go wrong?"

In asking these questions, in following the Judasvoice as it appeared in words before my eyes, I tried to deal with, or let Judas deal with the idea of intention or purpose or ambition, children, a notion of love, history, apostles, you, money, sex, selfhood, Some Lads, politicians and politics, and the possibility that Judas may be the spirit of language, of poetry. This last section shocked me. Everybody knows that the literary world everywhere, be it Dublin, London, Paris, New York, or even Sidcup or Skibbereen, can be hate-riddled to an astonishing degree. I've heard people say, 'Poets are self-centred, malignant bastards, aren't they, really?' These same people frequently go on to say that it's a great wonder, and a paradoxical cause for gratitude, that such malignant, self-centred bastards are capable of producing 'such beautiful stuff'. The implication is that poetry is produced *in spite of* the nature of these 'self-centred, malignant' souls. *The Book of Judas* explores the possibility that "beauty" is produced *because* of it. Judas has a permanent residence on the human tongue. His potential vitality in every word known to us is incalculable, thrilling and fascinating. Who can fully trust the words out of any mouth, especially his own?

This scapegoat, critic of self and society, throws chronological time out the window. Before his ancestors arrived on the scene, he was. After the unborn will have ceased to exist, he'll be. As others arrive, exist and perish, he tholes. Time is merely a stage where his reticent yet theatrical spirit is repeated and refined as it continues to endure the stones of blame thrown by those who really know the score. If I'd stuck to chronology in this poem I'd have lost the voices of that spirit. By treating time in the ways a blamed person treats it, that is, with the ceaseless nervous agility of the accused-from-all-sides, the poem became open to the stimulating effects of that electricity which saves most thinking people from the pornography of labels. And the man could talk and mutter as he wished, or was compelled to. I have always associated unbridled, passionate muttering with freedom. There is something more attractively genuine in such mutterings than in most of the bland interchanges that go by the name of "communication". Wherever I see men and women furiously muttering to themselves in the streets of Dublin I am saddened by their loneliness, touched by their sincerity, awed by their freedom.

I would like to thank Terence Brown for his readings of this poem and suggestions concerning it. Thanks also to Gerald Dawe for his reading and comments. And finally my gratitude to Neil Astley for his many ideas on how to shape and re-shape this work. It was he, chiefly, who gave the poem whatever shape it can claim to have.

Tony Roche in turn has helped shape *The Little Book of Judas* from *The Book of Judas*. I have followed all his suggestions as to which poems should be saved from the original work, including the one I hadn't written which appeared by an act of *deus ex libris*. Others were added by me, or at Neil Astley's suggestion, including thirty poems not included in the original book (these have aster-isked titles), either because they were lost at the time or because I wrote them later.

BRENDAN KENNELLY

I. Do it

Lips

What words emigrate through these:

Promises threats salutations curses lies
Protestations of love and hate
Memories wording to new shapes
Attempts at prayer
Cant and ranting
Money-counting
Enraged obscenities.

They work in my sleep.
I lie there, lost and vulnerable,
No longer in control.
The words escape into the darkness
Like hunger-strikers finding the gates open
Or cries from children swallowing hunger
On a mountain of excrement and death.

If I have a soul they tell it.
If I have a heart they let you know it.
Do they?

How often have they betrayed me
And told my little truth. Have they?

When I see trout flashing through water
They close in wonder.
When my blood is chill with anger
They are po-faced diplomats.
When I see pictures that make heaven a possibility
They ooze platitudes like spittle.
When I see precision bombers at work
They suck horror like mother's milk.

They think
Food and drink.
They breathe
Distinctions of stink.

They murder with chuckles and outbursts
Of laughter laughing at innocence.
They make hell what it is –
Ordinary, polished with commonsense.
They operate like a surgeon or a shark.
They electrify her body in the dark.

When they utter the beautiful words of others
They sneer at their own skill.

They listen. They lie in wait, daylight
Assassins.

They kill at will.
They kiss when pressed.

They subvert the moon's truest tunes,
They whistle music inside out
Making doubt certain, certainty doubt.

They permit pain to find a voice.
They stiffen when no one listens.
They freeze in the presence of what sees through them.

More than anything else
They understand silence.

They taste it, licking themselves
Till they are wet enough for pain
To utter itself all over again.

They slave for me, ask nothing in return.
The harder they work the more I wonder
If I believe them.

Do It

Do it, I said, do it for sure,
What in hell are you waiting for?

You could sit around forever
Dreaming plotting scheming thinking
Sensitively festering, saying

      I want to change the situation
      I want others to see the change
      I want unborn eyes to see the difference
      I want you to see how destructive you are
      When you love and pray
      And lead the ignorant natives astray
      And save the animals from death

      I want to scrub dead gratitudes
      Clarify the bitter feuds
      Burn the murderous plans
      To help the vulnerable children

      I want to shred every mind
      That ever dreamed of money

      Money

      I want to know that I am here

      – Not a leaf in the wind
      Not a dead neighbour nor yesterday's headlines
      Not the slitting words of a busy cynic
      Nor a political speech at some self-acclaiming conference

      Not a girl's bloodgush in her growing
      Not a shrunken hope
      Nor a dogsvomit despair

      And I don't want to turn away
Into a home a job a bank a promise
A weekend retreat

A night
With the most fabulous little fucker in the land

And Jesus is she great

And I don't want to make a statement
Or write a poem
Or paint a picture
Or hack a shape from stone
Or win a prize for the skilled quality of my lies

I want to do it
And I will I will

It's only what the me-me world deserves

Just give me a second to steady my nerves

Service

The best way to serve the age is to betray it.
If it's a randy slut slooping for hump
Hide in a dark ditch, wait, waylay it
And land where no one can extradite you.

If it's a moneyman with a philosophy like
'There's only cash and as many fucks as you can get'
Inspire him to talk of Daddy's tenderness
Till his eyes are wet.

Be a knife, bullet, poison, flood, earthquake;
Cut, gut, shrivel, swallow, bury, burn, drown
Till someone senses things ain't as they should be.

If betrayal is a service, learn to betray
With the kind of style that impresses men
Until they dream of being me.

Insincerity as a Detector of Human Worth

Men have a passing interest in each other
Though only a few care about anyone else.
This does not prevent them seeing themselves
As lovers, and feeling love upon the pulse.

Such love is the perfect way not to know
Anyone, because of its fatal sincerity.
Marriages collapse because they're based on what's true
At the time. Fulfilment is another name for atrophy.

If on the other hand you experiment with lies
Salted with what is deftly insincere
You'll see their hearts as your words come and go.
Let them take the bait. Assume a wise
Look. Be hurt, if necessary. Say you're queer
Or a Jesusfreak. Their eyes will tell you all you
Need to know. What do you need to know?

Abraham's Bosom

I've died many times,
Not always because of well-conceived
And well-executed crimes
But because, being undeceived,
I glimpse a little, understand much
And hang myself
Out of a tingling mixture of boredom and shame.
The ninth time I died
I shot straight to Abraham's bosom,
A smelly place in West Heaven. I saw
Adam and Eve chatting about apples, Cain
And Abel editing a study of Brotherly Love,
Various Popes discussing greed lust envy pride
Hitler organising the resurrection of the Jews
Dante and Beatrice refusing to get out of bed.

'Welcome to my bosom, Judas' Abraham said,
'Despite your atrocious name I appreciate your worth.'

'I don't like your bosom, Abe' I replied
'It's too large, damp, unacceptably hairy.
I'm dropping back to earth.'

Back to this dear criminal dump I came
Glad of my good fortune, my bad name,
Sceptical of my next outing to Abraham's bosom.

Halcyon Days

I find the four gospels a darned good read
Though I don't come well out of the scene.
I saw what I saw, did what I did
And shed no tears over what might have been.

These were halcyon days, sane, insane,
Small farmers and fishermen leaving home
On impulse, just up and out, quick adventurous men.

I liked Peter, first Pope and Bishop of Rome.

Far from all that the same Peter was born and bred.
Leaving the wife and kids must have been hard
But Peter always did what Peter had to do.

In this, we were not unalike. I'm glad
These gospels show him in a kindly light.
I once wrote in my scrapbook that what I approve of I tend to
regard as true.

The Devil's Lilies

Seeing a cat crucified to a telegraph pole
The latest fast cars gulping the highways
I realise God created the world
In a psychedelic haze

I see the spaced-out heroes hacking
Each other to pieces in the scenic glens
While sprawled poets invent the Bible
In opium dens

Little remains for me but to set out again
After coffee on a contemplative stroll
Through timeless weeds and daffydowndillies,
My mind much like the minds of other men
From Bethlehem and Bradford and Listowel.
These men are flowerless. I pick the devil's lilies.

An O.K. Guy

So much depends on a TV appearance.
It's true it's true it's absurd.
I practised for days but clean
Forgot how my beard
Stuck like a watery turd to my chin
And what a seedy sneaky voice I have
And darting ratty eyes
Infecting the light of surburban paradise.
No one believed me, I was dressed in lies.
And yet in spite of these disasters
I might have come across as an OK guy
Were it not that at a vital moment
I picked my nose. The whole fucking nation
Rang the station and said I should be crucified.
Today a blob of snot on my forefinger
Recalls an agony on which I shall not linger.

In That Moment

There must have been a first time.
Something was broken, a grace lost,
A man sidestepped himself, a woman lied.

In that moment, persecution and martyrdom
Happened, two hearts learned not to trust,
A remarkable person was betrayed.

Beatification

When I was a Chat Show Host,
My nationwide programme
Approaching its nightly end,
I would suddenly up my interest
In the proceedings. Leaning
Towards the face of the most
Beautiful woman in the place,
I would say with an urgent air
'We have thirty seconds left!
Who, in your view, is the best
Chat Show Host in the colourful
History of television?'
The beautiful creature would hesitate
For one staggering moment
And explode,
'You, Judas, you alone, you are God!'
The nation swilled her words.
I, angelically bright,
Kissed ten million hearts good-night
From My undisputed place,
Smiling as a blush of modesty
Beatified my face.

On Board *

I steered my boat between the rocks
Over the bad gravel and the wicked stones
Over the stories of girls' suicides
And drowned men's bones
            To the place where the sun
Danced on the troubles of us all
Not giving a tinker's curse
If we were still keeping body and soul

Together, or apart.
It was there I saw what I thought I wanted.
I leaned out
Over the side of the boat and tried
To take the concept on board
But I missed and it sank slowly out of sight.
Centuries later, I'm grateful for that.
Why try to save a drowning rat?

Which Matters?

This had all the ingredients of an epic story:
A God, immortal beauty and power,
Perfect above deficient human machinery
Cranking away, keeping an obstinate grip on wonder,
Imagining itself for battle, leaving the heart open
To consequential attacks of passion.
We dreamed ourselves, dreams were the lives of men,
When lives were dreamed how real were hell and heaven.
            But even as I defined the cosmos
I ceased to tell the story and became
Interested in myself, self-seeking, what my feelings were.
Friendships frayed, I liked each new neurosis,
Sticky confessions whimpered my way to fame,
The scene splattered apart in rags and tatters.
Epic story? Whimpering scene? Which matters?

II. Are the poems honest, doctor?

Appetite

Collecting urine-samples in outer Rathmines
In the name of Church, country and God
Became my duty when I was made
Head of the Vice-Squad
Sniffing out heroin and synthetic-opiate addicts
In the heart of the Supermarket jungle.
These ravenous children, victims from the womb, sick
And ecstatic, are mad
For money as farmers, darlings of Mummy Earth.
        Like a virtuous Revenue Officer
So contemptuous of fame
No slippery victim will ever know my name,
        I ferret them out,
        Drag them into the light
Where they skeletonstand, chewed by their own appetite.
        These are the true poets,
        Each one
Skilled in the art of self-crucifixion,
        Hung up on
Spoofy proofs of self-fabrication,
        Mangy angels of smelly damnation,
        Freak dreams of an ego
        Shivering in a doorway
        Lousy with lyricism,
        No end to their lust
Only the patient, wearing, heartless, absolute,
        Brotherly, smothering, vindictive
        Pity of dust.

The Distinct Impression

'I was delivering a child
In this kip of a bedroom in Keogh Square.
The woman jerked and groaned in the bed
Sweat wetting her hair.

Six children lumped and stared at me
As I worked on her.
In the bed with the woman was her man,
Face to the wall, an occasional snore.

"Is it out yet?" he asked of a sudden.
If I'd a bucket o' boilin' water then
I'd have emptied it over his skin.

I had the distinct impression
That the moment the child was out of the woman
That bastard would be back in.'

Eily Kilbride

On the North side of Cork city
Where I sported and played
On the banks of my own lovely Lee
Having seen the goat break loose in Grand Parade

I met a child, Eily Kilbride
Who'd never heard of marmalade,
Whose experience of breakfast
Was coldly limited,

Whose entire school day
Was a bag of crisps,
Whose parents had no work to do,

Who went, once, into the countryside,
Saw a horse with a feeding bag over its head
And thought it was sniffing glue.

A Pit of Dead Men

Dr Bridgeman said 'What are we to do
If ten-year-old poets insist
On writing of these midnight meetings
With their fathers' lust,
     Randy shaggers invading their daughters' beds
Trying to hush the whole thing up at the same time?
The daughters are writing about it, using their heads,
Telling the world of their fathers' crimes,
Keeping nothing back, all spilled out, can you imagine
What it'll do to these families?

When I was at school we did Shakespeare and Milton,
I learned *Paradise Lost* and all its epic beauties,
Adam and Eve and God, Heaven, Hell and Satan
But these children's poems stink like a pit of dead men.'

'Are the poems honest, Doctor? Should the young girls tell?'

'What good is honesty if home is hell?'

Night Air

'My friend Rebecca returned from a party,
Glad of the peace of home, sat in
Her living-room listening to music.
After a while she decided to check the children,
Softly upstairs towards Jonathan's bedroom.
He was twelve, her favourite. She found him
Lying in bed, naked, asleep, his penis
Erect in the light thrown from the landing.
Before she knew it she was at the bedside,
Wanting the boy's penis inside her. Breathing
"Jonathan! Jonathan!" she leaned towards him, then realising
Herself, turned, closed the door, rushed downstairs, out
Into the garden, gulped the night air, her shocked mind shivering.'

Ancient Surprise *

Girl in a pink anorak caresses a swan
With her eyes, under the Happy Holidays ad.
       A lyric moment, nothing bad
Can mar it, then why does it seem to me betrayed
       Quickly as I perceive it?
Has it to do with the tale of the ten-year-old
Girl in this morning's letter – how a man whose father
I knew and loved for he was pure gold
Destroyed her in ways I'd rather not mention here?
   I go beyond the girls to the woman
Who has found Christ. O sweet Mary Lowe
How do you do, now that heaven's on your side?

       Happy, most happy, dear Judas. I do the summer season
In Blackpool, adore the Christmas Panto,
And with God for a guide, smile like this morning's bride.

Good luck, Mary Lowe. While you travel on
I see a girl in a pink anorak caressing a swan
With her eyes.
For the moment, no kisses, no kissing lies.
This is a healthy, ancient surprise.

Children's Rage *

Will you listen to your children when they ask
'Who killed the river?'
Will you turn your head away and say
You lost your memory
After you came back from Africa
Where you'd lain three months
With a jungle fever?

Will you listen to your children when they ask
'Why was Vinnie Greene compelled to steal?'

27

Will you stick your nose into a book and say
You lost interest in people
When killing seemed inevitable
So you decided to relax and see
If stupid wounds would heal.

Will you say –
                        'This is a harmful age,
A man must protect himself.'
How will you protect yourself
                        From children's rage?
Children are people who refuse
To let their courage age.

Cardboard Child

As I sniffed my way through the midnight smoggy
I saw children sleeping
In doorways of the rubbishy city –
Almost enough to set me weeping.
I approached a cardboard child and asked
'Why are you not at home in bed?'
'No home,' she said 'No home', again and again.
She lay like a litterbag
Near the river thickening to the sea.
No champion of justice I, yet I swear
Rare rage boiled up. I was wild.
'The wrong people,' I said, 'own all the silver,
All the silver.' She looked at me. She didn't care.
What do I care for the cardboard child?

I'll Crawl Into Her Heart *

The girl has hanged herself in the cell
Yet all is well yes all is well
And she has left a prayer
Hanging there in the quite
Indifferent light:

> *O God I am alone.*
> *It's hard to feel*
> *That anyone cares*
> *Including you, O God.*
>
> *Help me to believe*
> *You are my friend.*
> *How can anyone*
> *Understand?*
>
> *I don't want to be*
> *Filled with hate.*
> *I've seen too much hate.*
> *I don't want to eat hate anymore.*
>
> *Forgive me please*
> *For what I've done.*
> *Help me*
> *To live again.*

Her fourteen years are hanging there.
What do I care?
Was she a cardboard child?
If she'd lived
Would she be a cardboard woman?

> *Help me to believe*
> *You are my friend.*
> *How can anyone*
> *Understand?*

Understand? I'll crawl into her heart to-night
And hang myself for fun
Or spite.

words

what's words ozzie assed me
sounds dat kum outa peepul's mouths i said
where dey kum from first sez ozzie
dunno i replied

fukken fish have no words ozzie went on
but dey enjoy de fukken sea
and fukken tigers have no words
but dey enjoy eatin you and me

only peepul has words ozzie said
an luk at de shit dey talk
if i kud reed i'd say buks are shit as well

words are to kummyunikate sez i

like shit sez ozzie won good bomm
blow de whole fukken world ta hell

prades

ozzie is stonemad about prades
so he say kummon ta belfast
for de 12th an we see de orangemen
beatin de shit outa de drums
beltin em as if dey was katliks' heads

so we set out from dublin
an landed in belfast for de fun
it was brill
dere was colour an music an everyone
was havin a go at sumtin i dunno

what but i'll never forget ozzie in
de middul of all de excitement
pickin pockets right left and centre

on de train back to dublin he was laffin his head
off, dere shud be more fukken prades he said

flushed

ozzie kum to me all flushed sez he
i want a fukken ride
i was lukken at de telly lass nite
sumwun played here kums de bride

sum fukken bride i can tell ya boy
i very nearly hopped inta de box
kummon now sez ozzie we'll go ta
our pub down de keys an get our rocks

off so down we toddle like a pair
o' young bulls up from de cuntry

fifteen pints o' cider a man i never lied
about drink in me life we pick up two
fine tings an screw em crosseyed up in de park
ozzie said tis hard ta whack de fukken ride

skool

dis jesus fella sez ozzie who was he
how de fuck do i know sez i
you went ta skool forra bit sez ozzie
didn't learn much dayre sez i

but he died on de cross sez i
for you an for me de teetchur said
what de fuck you talkin about sez ozzie
de man is dead dat's all de man is dead

but everywun sez jesus dis an jesus dat
pay de jesus rent by us a jesus pint
till i get de jesus dole

but who de jesus hell was he sez ozzie
i dunno sez i yoor jesus iggerant sez he
shuv yoor iggerance up yoor bleedin hole

31

Jobs

'Me first mistake was stealin' two bob
Off me daddy. If I'd a bit o' common
Jimmy Rafferty I'd a told him straight
But I hedged an' he hit me an' got me a job

As a messenger-boy in a shop in Duke Street,
I stuck it for two years, then I went workin'
For a cloth-maker shoulderin' rolls
O' cloth all over me city o' Dublin, sweatin'.

Left that, too. Lugs Brannigan gave me a cuff
On the ear one night when I crashed a queue
Outside the Odeon, then got me a job as an usher.
Lugs was a great man, helped the poor

Especially women beaten by animalmen.
I left that too. At nineteen I started to drink
Porter Phoenix Carlsberg Smithwicks Power Jameson

Anything then. Then I stopped it,
Got a job in the sewers. With
Helmet gloves rubber clothes flashlamp
I went down below Dublin

From Kingsbridge into O'Connell Street
Flashin' me lamp in the eyes o' rats
Diabolical as tomcats. Rats don't like light
In their eyes. I waded through shit,

Women's jamrags and men's rubbers stuck
To my rubbery clothes. Rubber clings to rubber.
The ends men will go to for a fuck!
The sewers o' Dublin are flush with the relics o' lovers.

Motherogod, what flowed between me legs!
I left that too, I wrote a song and a hymn
Called *My Lady in Blue*
I wanted Micky Mocke to sing it, that fell through,

I have four grandchildren now, I love 'em, I'm fifty-five,
I've a security job, I'm happy, I'm workin', I'm alive.'

Herod's Way

Herod's way of coping with children?
'Knife the little fuckers, one by one.'

The Little Trick

So much to say, so little said.
The children's souls are roses after rain.
I think tonight of the world's dead –
        Suppose they lived again

And saw the consequences of their attempts to be
Fathers and mothers to the likes of me.
Let me not dwell on that, the story
Is of men or monsters, have it your way.

Even if I said what I have to say
It'd be a lie in the end, long before the end,
One word after another, tale, song, poem, lie;

I must operate on myself, the question is how.
Do I apply the knife and find
The little trick that makes me live or die?

Or admit my words betray my pain,
Throw pennies at them, tinkers in the rain?

Murty's Burning Hands

I heard the questions gunning past
Like assassins in search of a target.
I thought of Murty Galvin in the slow class,
The sweat on his forehead unable to answer
And Murty shaking at

Why did God make hell?
What do you mean by angels?
What is Original Sin?
On what day did God become man?
Where was Christ's body while his soul was in Limbo?
What is the greatest of all misfortunes?
What is forbidden by the ninth commandment?
For what end did God make us?
What is the happiness of heaven?

When the questions got no answer
Murty was beaten by the teacher.
'Take me to the fountain,' Murty said.
I pumped the water over Murty's burning hands.
He dried his hands on his jumper.
Whinbushes blazed madyellow, God knows why.
There was money for hares that must escape or die.
'All the fuckin' questions,' Murty said.
'An' me without an answer in me head.'

Feed the Children

Let my story feed the children
Who need a monster to hate and fear.
Arrange them in a classroom
Pour me into each innocent ear.
Be sure they know exactly what I've done
How I inflicted my own punishment
On myself, in a ropey place, alone.
Describe my face, my hands, my hair. Say I was sent
By darkness to commit the ultimate crime
Against the light and am the only man
Other men have not forgiven.
Tell the children all this, and more, so that their time
On earth will prove to all how no one
Of my kind can get within an ass's roar of heaven.

Tricks

The problem with having a dog is kids
I'm hearing noises I never heard before
Sure you could be killed crossin' the street
Must get in touch with Mary's organisation
Install a Chubb Alarm over the front door

When people speak of a victim
They have in mind
A frail elderly lady
With bad arthritis and partly blind

They rarely think of a strong brute like me
Strolling along a street
When two knife-wielding muggers attack
Grab all my cherished pieces of silver
Give me a valedictory stab in the back.

My mind is playing tricks, my bedsit is an abyss.
I'll see someone hangs for this.

Vigil

'The lady of the house is a notorious drug-pusher
The police know she's been at it for years
Our vigil at her door is to persuade her
To get out of here.
        I can't prove it but she killed my son.
It took him three years to die.
The lady has a husband two brothers a daughter and three sons:
A happy family
Planting misery in people, watching it grow
And deepen in the youngsters' eyes
While the lady of the house counts her money.
Why not call in the law, you ask. We tried that.
Whatever law is, it's in our hands now.
Law may be right and strong, law may be wise
But when a rat attacks me I kill the rat.'

Youngsters Today

'You can be sure o' nothin' now, sir.
You might get a knife in the chest or a hammer
On the head if you open the door to a stranger.
Young boys an' girls are stuck into crime, sir.

Mick Magee, an ould butty o' mine an' his sister
Julia, are livin' in a flat out in Cork Street.
Three girls, Legion o' Mary workers,
They said, knocked at their door. Mick and Julie

Greeted 'em heart-an'-a-half into the flat.
One o' the girls slipped upstairs, ransacked the place,
Stole every penny me friends'd managed to save.

Mick is arthritic, Julia's eyes are failin'.
D'you know what, sir? The youngsters today
Would steal a corpse outa the grave!'

III. I hear the pages crying

No Image Fits

I have never seen him and I have never seen
Anyone but him. He is older than the world and he
Is always young. What he says is in every ear
And has never been heard before.
I have tried to kill him in me,
He is in me more than ever.
I saw his hands smashed by dum-dum bullets,
His hands holding the earth are whole and tender.
If I knew what love is I would call him a lover.
Break him like glass, every splinter is wonder.
I had not understood that annihilation
Makes him live with an intensity I cannot understand.
That I cannot understand is the bit of wisdom I have found.
He splits my mind like an axe a tree.
He makes my heart deeper and fuller than my heart will dare to be.
He would make me at home beyond the sky and the black ground,
He would craze me with the light on the brilliant sand,
He is the joy of the first word, the music of the undiscovered human.
Undiscovered! Yet I live as if my music were known.
He is what I cannot lose and cannot find
He is nothing, nothing but body and soul and heart and mind.

> So gentle is he the gentlest air
> Is rough by comparison
> So kind is he I cannot dream
> A kinder man
> So distant is he the farthest star
> Sleeps at my breast
> So near is he the thought of him
> Puts me outside myself

> So one with love is he
> I know love is
> Time and eternity
> And all their images.
> No image fits, no rod, no crown.

> I brought him down.

Exception *

The last thing in this world
Anyone I know
Would dare to be
Is wholly free.

That is, of course, with the exception
Of one man,
One man alone.

See what happened to him.

Stretcher Case

What they think is love is not what love is.
Every thought is an act of Judas and a plea to Christ
Or an act of Christ and a plea to Judas
Whose heart was never iced

Over like the seminary in our town
During the no-go winter of sixty-three.
The milk froze in the cows;
Dreams in folks' heads, waves on the living sea

And the Great Philosophical Tradition were cramped
As an aging footballer who can't handle extra time
So the young winger blots him out,
The St John's Ambulance men stretcher him off.
He knows it's the end and the end is no shame
Because he gave it all he had for as long as he could.
What more can a stretcher-case do? Cover his head.
Supporters will tell you he loved what he did.
'A broken back? Jesus, he was a game kid!'

God As An Unmarried Mother

God fell in love with this Limerick fella
Who, although a good Confraternity Man,
Fell in love with God also
And wanted to have a baby with Her.

It happened one night in a field outside Glin.
God got pregnant and the Confraternity Man
Changed because he re-fell in love with the old sin-
stuff. God was left on Her own.

God gave birth to a darling child
And struggled to rear him all by Herself.
Some people were kind but quite a few condemned Her

Writing to the papers to say She was defiled
And deserved to be left on the shelf
By the Confraternity Man who was safe in England somewhere.

A Moment of Love

Should I permit myself a moment of love
It would be for the way
He explodes in the face
Of dominant mediocrity
                        – a bomb of a man
Ticking in the timid corners of time.
     Is he the first terrorist
Warring against all that I am?

I am forcing my heart to open to the fact
That of all those I've known and half-known
He's the one who refuses to hide

Anything. Terrifying. He must be attacked
From all angles, get him, do him, he's the one
To be shot knifed hanged strangled drowned crucified.

We'll praise him when he's dead
Honour the truth of every word he said
Make his name inseparable from the name of God.

Holiday

It was years later, I was on holiday,
Late Autumn, one of my favourite towns
In the south-east corner of Africa,
Doing research in rare monkeys' skeletons.

I was strolling down a crowded street
Musing in that warm style, nostalgic and dim,
When (I swear to God my heart missed a beat)
I saw him

Passing about seven yards to my right side,
Looking straight ahead, clothed in white,
Calm, purposeful, tall.

I stared, then ran through the crowd,
Touched his shoulder, blurted my question straight.
'Sorry' he smiled, 'Sorry. That's not my name at all.'

I froze back to rare monkeys' skeletons, human fool.

The Beautiful Sentiments

The beautiful sentiments comfort me like Johnson's
Babypowder motherkissing my skin.
I could cry when I hear 'Love thy neighbour',
Secret of home, civilisation.

Yet my neighbour is less than loving
Saying and doing things not greatly to my taste
Such as expecting me to breakfast on
Choice cutlets of nuclear waste.

For behold my neighbour dumpeth his opulent waste on me
Oozing like fat tributes from his poison-palaces
Humming with good works in his unmean and pleasant land.
How shall I love this neighbour who murders the sea
And in murdering it propagates oily lies?
My love, I fear, turns sour. Will my neighbour understand?
My neighbour. Neighbour. Might I not spend
An average dicey winter
Brooding on that word? Nay! Burr!
No. Neighbour. Who is my neighbour?
After two thousand years on earth, I ask
Who is my neighbour? Lost God, let me choose
One, he was blind, his brother had the task
Of guiding him down the village street to Mass
Where he, blind and slight, gazed at the tabernacle.
That's where God is, the priest and teacher said.
House of Gold
            Ark of the covenant
                    Morning Star
Remember o most tender...so blind and small,
My neighbour's words were eyes, eyes blind with blood,
He died, his brother died, my mind is where they are,
If I forget or banish them, they never were,
If the fierce dream weakens, I have no neighbour,
If I have no neighbour, I am no lover,
If the fierce dream weakens, I am loveless ever.

I Hear the Pages Crying

'My dear Ted, I followed him
For several years through the country
Trying to keep track of his parables and miracles,
His love mercy pity
For the most leprous types this place can produce.
I watched him closely, taking regular notes.
I looked at him looking
Into people's hearts, sifting their minds,
Giving them gifts of light, hearing and sight.
I listened to the voices of his friends and enemies.
I decided to write.

I've been busy with my own work, it's not easy
Being a country G.P.
But I think I caught something of him
Or did I half-catch the merest glimpses?
It's hard to say, the book seemed to write itself,
Had to be there, a cat cleaning itself in the sun,
A knowledge that flesh is mercy covering the bone,
Becoming its own history, its own mythology.
He was heartbreakingly human, I won't write again,
There is no language that is not in vain,
No beautiful line that is not profane,
Ignorance showers through my heart and brain
Like this endless sickness in men women children,
My book stinks of sickness, a sweaty sense of dying
Into the notion that truth becomes helpless lying,
He moved through that, I tried for the right words,
They twisted, gibbered, where are the words for him?
At every sickbed now I hear the pages crying.'

My Mind of Questions

Did Jesus have brothers and sisters?
        Did they give him a rough time?
What was it like on a Saturday night
        In the Holy Family home?

Did they mock his God-like talents?
        Laugh at wise things he said?
Did he fight with them for an extra spud
        Or a cut o' brown bread?

Did he have a favourite sister
        Who understood him better than most
And agreed that he was the Father
        Son and Holy Ghost?

If challenged, would he fight back,
        Square up to a bully?
Was he a handy lad with the mitts
        Sidestepping beautifully

When a bigger lad charged at him,
        Expecting to knock him down?
Did Jesus trip him up
        Then go to town?

What was he like in the scrap
        When the dirt blinded his eyes?
Did he ever get a kick in the balls
        From some frigger twice his size?

When, in the streets of Nazareth,
        Did he first hear the name of God?
Did he know it was his own name
        When he first tasted blood?

Did he go in search of birds' nests
        In meadow, field and glen?
And if he found a thrush's nest
        Did he rob it then?

Did he ever fish for eels
        And watch them die at his feet
Wriggling like love in the dust?
        Gospels, you're incomplete.

What was he like at school?
        Was he fond of poetry?
Did he make the teacher feel like a fool
        Because he lacked divinity?

What did the teacher think of him
        Doing his father's business?
Did he wonder at times if Jesus
        Was out of his tree, or worse?

Did Jesus like to sing?
        Did he whistle and hum
As he walked the streets of Nazareth
        Going home to mum?

(I've heard it said he lacked
        A sense of humour,
That his mind was grim and grew grimmer
        And grimmer and grimmer).

What was his appetite like?
　　　　What did he like to eat?
What did he see the first time he washed
　　　　His hands and feet?

What were his fingers like? His mouth?
　　　　His throat, toes, thighs, teeth, eyes?
Did he often cry? For what? And what
　　　　Was the sound of his sighs

At night when he was alone
　　　　And no one had ever been created
Except as shadowy strangers
　　　　Who went their separate ways?

What did he think of his neighbours?
　　　　His neighbours of him?
Was he a quiet little fella
　　　　Fond of his home?

Or did he sometimes seem
　　　　As if he were biding his time
Like a man with a job to do
　　　　That took up all his mind?

At what moment did he know
　　　　That home is not enough
And he must scour the darkness
　　　　To give and find love

Among strangers waiting out there
　　　　Full of need,
So full his heart inclined
　　　　To bleed?

Did he break up his family?
　　　　Did they resent him?
From the day he left did he ever
　　　　Get in touch again?

Was he handsomely made
　　　　Or humped, mis-shapen?
Was his life a preparation
　　　　For what can never happen?

44

When he saw the sadness of sex
           Did he sit and think
Or slip down a Nazareth laneway
           For a happy wank?

Back in the Holy Family
           All hope and despair on the shelf
Did he look in the eyes of others
           Or smell himself?

Did he stand in a doorway of time
           Look at a street
Hear people bawl for his blood
           And then forget

He'd ever existed? Did he shudder
           To know the future now?
Did he know? How could he bear it?
           The sweat on the boy's brow

Turns to blood in my mind of questions,
           How foolish they are,
What do I know of anything,
           Even my own star?

My own star above all, perhaps?
           My own blood?
My own tracking, trackless, shapeless, restless,
           Sleepless head?

I Am Resolved

Jesus, I said, I do not swear, I am resolved,
No matter what blinds my eyes or blocks my way
Or ordains that my whole purpose be halved,
Not to let the clichés get in my way.

The first cliché is love. I tore a strip of his skin.
Look at this cliché, I said, was it for this you died?
Was it for this you dumped yourself in the loony-bin of sin?
Yes, he replied.

Strip by strip I peeled the clichés, bits of flesh,
Slivers of bone, then the vital mucky stuff.
Clichés, I said, clichés, is this all you have to give?
Why try to hide the fact of human trash?
Why not Hitler the bastards? Cut up rough?
What am I to do with the clichés since
Every cliché is prepared to say what it means to live?

I'm not going to mention his reply.
You know it, anyway.

A Pleasant Evening

I drove Jesus out to Restaurant Merry Bó
In my snappy little Volkswagen (secondhand).
Starters were good: Jesus had avocado
With prawns while I chose courgette soup and
Bacon with croutons. For the main course
Jesus took vinegared cod, filleted by the Merry Bó
Boss himself, there at the table. Steak with butter and herb

Sauce was my melt-in-the-mouth choice. The
Dessert trolly brought chocolate mousse and
Lemon soufflé. We scoffed the lot, God help us.
The house wine was good, a real presence on our lips.
The bill was reasonable, a mere thousand. I
Paid. A pleasant evening, given our relationship.
Driving home, we agreed that eating is an art.
Jesus released the occasional fart.
Later on, I Merrion Squared and got laid.
All that womanthing. All that Volkswagen. All that food.

Saturday

On Friday, the nailing and cutting-down of the God.
On Sunday, the rising up.
What happened on Saturday?

Feeling a sudden brain-spasm
I sat down that Saturday to study
The Church of Ireland Historical Catechism
With a Foreword by the Most Rev. Arthur W. Barton, D.D.

I discovered Queen Elizabeth the First
Took lessons in Irish Grammar from a book
By Lord Devlin. Storing the Lord's Grammar in her head
She sent Irish type to Dublin
That Bibles and books be printed
To bring good Christian luck to all.
That was the most erudite Saturday of my life.
On Sunday, God rose from the dead.

Lambs for Good Friday Dying *

The Curlew Skibber laughed and cut
The throat of another lamb,
He liked the blood of innocence
And stayed an innocent man.

Innocent slaughtering innocent
Is a perplexing sight,
The Curlew ate what the Curlew killed
And enjoyed good sleep at night.

The Curlew's wife saw his bloody hands
And brought him soap and water
To scour himself like a son of man
That they might live together

Happy in blood and beasty crying,
Lambs for Good Friday dying.

Handclasp

The first time we met we shook hands,
He looked me in the eyes, I knew
He'd never patted anyone on the back,
My favourite odious gesture. No

Handclasp in my experience resembled this,
Unutterably different from all I'd known.
Handclasps teach more than Universities,
Are shocking revelations of men

And women. I know a politician whose clasp
Is like babyshit, a Civil Servant's
That makes me wish to vomit, bomb, let rip

But I don't, never; an academic's that suggests
A Ph.D. in spartan wanking. But this was different.
I loved that handclasp, that quick, visionary grip.

Open Your Hearts

Open your hearts to the Holy Spirit
For Christ's sake.
We'll be back to you in a moment
After this commercial break.

IV. History

Grey Ashes, Black Ashes

Death in Bellefeast, seagulls screaming,
I saw all the books ever written
Sprouting wings in the thoughtless morning,
All the writers long forgotten
Moving fingers done with moving.

Books flew to a darkness between two stars
The earth and I were the last spectators
One by one the books became fire
The darkness laughed as the flames leaped higher

And higher until only ashes
Drifted away:

    Grey ashes of thought, black ashes of feeling
Started to fall on the fields and cities
Where people had given words their allegiance
Till black and grey ashes began falling, falling.

I'm back where I started, the taste of nothing,
Death in Bellefeast, seagulls screaming.

When I Look

When I look south I see greed
And muck in their peasant eyes
When I look east I see creeps
And conmen and chatterboxes
When I look west I see bull-necked
Wranglers refusing to pay their way
When I look north I see murder
And money and cute hooks fishing the sea.
Now is the time to make east become west
South become north and so on until each
Curse-o'-God shagger becomes another.

This should make the desert blush with interest
Open new sympathies for tadpole and cockroach
Unleash the mystical possibility that I am
Your sister and you are my brother.

Bags

The first bag of griefs he hoisted on his back
Was the griefs of children, a sound of playing
Mingled with cries. The second bag
Across his shoulders was the griefs

Of women. Sighs first, then screams flayed
The sacking, all was still for a while.
The third bag of griefs was the griefs of men
Or those who dreamed they were men, their style

Of suffering authentic through centuries.
This was a bag of pictures, including one
Of a man seeing himself in another's eyes before

Killing him, scurrying on into another picture,
Then another, heavy bags on the shoulders of one man
But voices from all the bags cried 'There are more! There are more!'

My Production Notebook

To get a proper understanding of the event
Which I foresaw would matter much to men
Though few among them grasped what it meant
I kept a production notebook on the crucifixion.

I wanted, above all, to get the details right.
For example, the precise structure and weight of the cross
Involved concentrated study late into the night.
I did several drawings of the nails, this was

Fascinating work, I chose samples of the mob's faces,
I noted exactly how the hammers fitted into
The honest fists of those who drove the nails home

For a pittance. To grasp the drama, my production notebook
Is vital. You may consult it at the University
Of Texas: they bought it for an undisclosed sum.

It Slipped Away

One day I saw a zebra
Accept a tiger's fangs.
I saw the tiger eat his fill
Though he didn't gorge himself as humans do.

And one day I saw a virgin
Accept a refusal of her invitation to love.
                        Her face turned grey,
She broke aside, into herself, wept a little
When her might-have-been lover went his way.

        And I too accepted something
Of which I find it difficult to speak.
For a moment, I accepted God's blessing
On my own calling as a traitor.
        I knew the meaning of happiness then
But it slipped away like a never-again-heard song
Beautiful to remember, beyond all right and wrong.

Hungers

I took the battered century in my arms
And kissed its lips and kissed its eyes and said
'Too well I know the Trojan Worms
Waiting for you, old son, bowed under blood,
Withered with loneliness, stupid with noise,
Your veins caked with politics.

51

Near the top of that cliff-face
A seagull manages to feed her young
Ignoring the poison brownfoaming the shore,
Thickening the air. Everywhere
The greedy, elegant monsters grow strong,
Twisted children die or live as cripples
Sprawled like stricken birds in a pity of bridges,
The dead moan in our hearts but tell us nothing
Or we have forgotten how to listen.
Your belly is full of war and death and money.'

The sad battered century said, 'I wanted you to live
But killing is your way and then a rest from killing
And then killing again. Child, lies are your food
And lies will make your heart beat strong and proud
And prompt you to discover worlds
You scarcely dare to dream of now.
And still you will not learn from the seagull.'

The battered century sighed and seemed to sleep.
I covered it and left it there
And walked where squawking hungers ripped the air.

I was a face, the kind you know must care.

A Scattering of Hay

I go back to the stable this winter night.
The door coughs open, I edge into the darkness,
Stand still. Somewhere, an old woman
Is shouting in a drunken voice,

        'Every mother's son in this accursed place
Has to go to a foreign country to make a livin'.
This bloody hell is a curse-o'-God disgrace.'

She stops, whimpering. I hear a bottle smashing
Against a wall. My eyes search the darkness.
Opposite me, near a corner, lies a cow,
Sleeping, I think. Men's voices blur from the road.

I move slowly over to where the manger is,
I put my hand in the manger, there's only
A scattering of hay, I feel cold and sad,
The feeling passes, I stand in the dark a while.
Nothing, no sound but the cow's breathing, calm and even.
Men I have drunk and yarned with would smile
To see me here, standing, they'd say, on the floor of heaven.

Taste

Now that I know the taste I've longed for
All my days, I think of the first time
I tasted Marina's kiss in the ruin of the Nor-
man Keep. Honey is acrid by comparison.

I remember the first time I tasted blood,
My own, a sunny field, June day, a swinging
Right cross from Francis Ignatius Wade,
Self-taste flooded my being.

And then for years I thought of the taste of evil:
Would it be the flesh of an enemy on my tongue?
Would I eat my enemy? Make a meal of the curse?
Feel at home forever at table with the devil?
I tasted it last night. I must write you a long
Letter about it sometime. It was bad. I've known worse.

A White, Empty Room

'I'm happy to be home, I can't believe
I'm back safe and sound with my wife and children.
I was walking along High Street
When they swept me into a car
        And drove to an outlying Station.
They locked me in a white, empty room
For seventy-two hours. You did it you did it
They repeated until I began to believe I was

Guilty. I'd never felt such guilt before.
You're a murderous thug, they said,
Shouting through every bone in my head,
You'll never see your family again
You'll get life you'll be hanged that's for sure.
Why did they suddenly release me then?
I was guilty no I'm not guilty now I know I'm not.
I've never even seen the place where Cassidy was shot.'

A Woman Is Bleeding

A woman is bleeding in my sleep: up
To me now she flows and says 'Do you desire
The blood of my eyes to challenge your eyes
Or do you wish me to bleed into a cup,

Hand it to you to throw at the bully
Screw in Block Four?
If he has the right kind of break in his skin
This cup o' blood will hurt him for sure.

Or do you want to lie with me here,
Fly down with me now in my blood?
We'll be all one then like the homeless people
In the streets of ice, our blood will give them shelter,
Even the cold churches will offer heat and food,
Let me bleed into you, or live sly, dry and unbridgeable.'

Initiation Rite

Whenever you find a group in society
Which feels that what it's doing
Is seriously different from any
Other group you get the kind of thing

I was subjected to when I joined
The apostles. My initiation rite:
I was hosed with cold water
And dumped in the street

In a babydoll nightdress, I was pelted
With stones and gassed with CS,
My private parts daubed with indelible ink

I was handcuffed to railings through a freezing night
And had my naked buttocks lashed with a baseball bat.

These humbling treatments did me some good, I think.

Apparition

He stretched there ready to be nailed
But we couldn't find anyone to finish the job.
We put ads in all the national papers,
Radio and telly, looking for someone who'd

Grab the hammer and home the nails.
Nobody came forward. I thought
We'd have to let him stand up and walk away
Laughing at the plight
Of us who'd seen the light.

Then, when all seemed lost, Flanagan
Apparitioned. He asked about the fee,
Pondered, said 'I'll do it! Where's the hammer?'

                    Flanagan gave it all he had.
Afterwards, he vanished with the money
Eschewing all display of bravado or glamour.

Gralton

The priest was loud.
'Follow Gralton or follow Christ!' he roared,
'Good people of Drumsna, remember our Lord
And the way he died for all men.
Gralton is a socialist.
Socialism is another name for communism.
Is it Christ or Gralton in transcendent Leitrim?'

'Gralton, by Christ!' an old man said.

Gralton escaped to New York. One night
He found a beggar in the streets, took him home,
Gave him food and drink, a bed.

When Gralton woke the beggar was gone.
So were Gralton's money and clothes.
Not for the first time Gralton was naked.

Like Myself

A thousand years later, they stripped me naked,
Flung me face downwards on the floor.
In this position I was held by several men
While others flogged me with cords stiffened
In melted pitch. My flesh piecemealed
At every stroke until my back was one
Large ulcer. Believe me, it was no joke.
Also, my brothers, I was miserably afflicted
With a beastly plague of gnawing vermin
Crawling in lumps within, without, about my body,
Hanging in clusters from my beard, lips, nostrils
And previously stylish eyebrows, blinding me.
Areta, the silver platekeeper, true to his cruel ways,
Gathered and swept the vermin upon me twice in eight days.
Spirited exercise of intelligence was my only crime
But that's how aspiring heretics were treated at the time.

After Such Knowledge

One evening, chatting with the damned, I noticed
How satisfied they were.
For every question concerning the living and dead
They had the answer.
The damned are an expert lot
The damned are convincing and urbane
The damned are so erudite
They flush your bewilderment down the drain.

The damned are burning with insight
Into time and eternity, mystery and art
And the mind of God.

I saw my brothers there, I saw the light
Of learning illumine the dark places of my heart
And the secret prisons in my blood.

After such knowledge I am paralysed with gratitude.

Bagatelle

Jesus was divine, I felt diviner
Especially after I'd composed
My Judas Bagatelle in B Minor.
I noticed how my colleagues dozed

While he went aside to pray
To his father who is himself and someone else as well,
Who, I dare not say.

Knowing that sleeping can be hell
And criminally irresponsible
I embarked on my Bagatelle,
Finished it without an error.

I play it now for friends who sleep
When their creator kneels to pray and weep
For them, himself, and other victims of the terror.

The Ultimate Rat

Hosting a TV Chat Show
I interviewed God.
'Why did you create me?' I asked.
God's buttocks squirmed. 'I had to' He said
'I wanted the world to see the most
Treacherous get it has ever known.'
'Were you pleased with the result?' I probed.
'Yes' answered God 'As men
Go, you are, you must admit, the ultimate rat
With a face like a bucketful of mortal sin.
You'd betray your own mother,
                              wouldn't you, my son?'

'I suppose I would' I mused as I flashed that
Winning Judasgrin. Viewers adored my honesty.
My tam-ratings soared high as heaven.

A Maligned Saint

At a gathering of the Christian churches
It was decided after long discussion
To conduct intensive research
Into my character, where I went wrong,
My special position in the human family.

In a comprehensive Gallup poll
Fifty million people were asked
'If you were judging Judas now
Would you show him any mercy?'

The result, excluding don't knows,
Showed I was not popular; but one person
Out of fifty million thought I was blessed,

A maligned saint. All the others said
I should be damned again and again.
Someone, somewhere, believed in me. Fuck the rest.

The Prize

I was awarded the Nobel Prize for Treachery
Just when I was beginning to feel
All my work had gone for nothing.
I'd begun to be slightly unreal
And could scarcely believe the tepid
Response to my adjustment of history
Though I know men are ignorant of what's happening
In them, about them. You can imagine my
Relief when the Great Minds dropped recognition
In my lap. I received fifty thousand pieces of silver
And an inscribed cup to commemorate my winning

The Prize. I bought a hideous Spanish Bungalow outside Skibbereen
Where I continue to meditate on the matter
Convinced, despite the éclat, my real work is only beginning.

Boom

'Know what I like, man? I like that big bomb
Some enlightened blighter will soon finger off
For the hell of it, just 'cos the bum
Feels his balls tickled by the notion of
                An exploding world
                Like the way I break
        Plates in the kitchen for old crime's sake.
And it'll get us all off the rack
Of each other's company, we'll just have one
                Final fuck
That won't get into the history-books –
            No forests, no paper, d'you understand?
To hell with forecasts, their measured gloom,
Spruce oracles of Government doom
In the box in the corner of the living-room,
                I want that bomb
                So the world shakes
And vanishes like a man into a woman
Going boom coming boom bloody boom boy boom.'

An Expert Lot

Dozens of international journalists
Attended the crucifixion.
An expert lot, they moved through the mob
    Doing the job, doing the job,
Collecting every scrap of the mob's reaction.
One whizzkid thought it might be a zippy idea
To interview Jesus on the cross
But Christ declined.
This was a tragic journalistic loss
Because the whizzkid had ready some very real
Questions, starting with 'Jesus, how do you feel?'
The television crews excelled themselves,
Slaves to the truth, sweated night and day
That every detail be revealed, the whole story told.
Even when the heavens darkened and the mountains coughed
And drops of blood became boiling rivers
    The cameras rolled.
Although the whizzkid failed to get an interview
With the Son of Man, he was undaunted
And managed to patch together
A programme that haunted the minds
Of millions who saw it on colour TV.
Some critics, however,
Protested at the silence of the central character.
What, they wanted to know,
Was his point of view?
Luckily for the whizzkid, he had a pal
On the staff of the Leading National Newspaper.
Pal, knowing sensitive whizzkid was shattered
By cruel reviews, arranged to set things right.
Discriminating viewers were quick to see the light
When they read The Only Review That Mattered.

Zone

No matter where I travel in my own little holy land
The buggers are after me, trying to prove
I changed forever the history of mankind
And flung in the gutter that immortal love
My master gave to every knacker scabbing the road,
Every robber leper killer pimp bandit whore thief
Insulting the face of heavenly god
With crimes I can hardly believe.

I'm the one who's wanted most. And now they intend
To set up The Hot Pursuit Of Judas Zone
For ten miles on either side of the border

Dividing me from my redeemer; but the bond
Between that man and me will go on and on
Despite church, state, stories of betrayal and murder.

I Was There

Sculpted columns, high ceiling,
Noon on Monday he'll be
Brought handcuffed to the court
When nine members of the jury
Are selected by lottery
From a group of thirty-five.
The court-clerk will take three hours
To read out the charges.

Joined the Movement at eighteen
Advised Latin-American dictators
On methods of interrogation.
Something of old Hollywood in his riding-crop.

Looks gentle as Saint Francis,
Benign old man, thin grey hair,
Sick from nervous disease
And a recent operation.

He will say
Certain national heroes were traitors
He will say
Moulin committed suicide
When he learned he'd been betrayed
By famous Resistance workers.
He will not apologise for his role as an officer.

He will say
He was a soldier doing dirty work
For the collaborationist government of the time
He will say
He is not guilty of a single crime.

He will ask
Why should he be tried
By those whose atrocities elsewhere
Have gone untried, unpunished?

He will play the tape
Again and again.

The Prime Minister is calling
For special lessons in schools
To trace the irresponsibilities of our fathers.

Other old men are gathering
In the shadow of the temporary monument
To speak of horrors more unspeakable
Than those at court.

The wizened butcher will listen to every word
His thin hands touching his thin hair.

He will say
That is not the whole story
That is not the whole story
I know
I asked questions of men and women
I organised the children
I followed instructions
I am your killer
I was there.

A Bag Like Everest

The way she turned what I said to her
Into something I wouldn't dream of saying!
She has a gift for changing a harmless murmur
Into a policy of betrayal.

                     The phone then –
'Wasn't it funny in print?'
Skibbereen Eagle, Squirish Mimes, Bethlehem News,
I'd read anything, looking for a hint,
A clue to the compulsive lies in language.

How many millions of lies are told every minute?
Child to father, man to woman, woman to man,
Lover to lover, friend to friend, worker to boss,
Boss to wife, wife to child, child to...?
                    My ambition is to get
A bag like Everest, collect all the lies in
The world and, packed bag on my back, walk
Through my brain beyond all treachery of talk
Until I find a cosy corner where
I can set my Everestbag on fire,
Brood on the blaze, see the pile of ashes grow
Like bonfires made by children long ago.

     Suddenly the wind works, the ashes rise
And scatter, self-born, spawning, countless clouds of lies.

Baby

In a nation where people are afraid
To go out at night
We must vote for men and women
Who're not afraid of an acceptable level of carnage.

It's time to clear Death Row.
Two hundred and forty prisoners are waiting to die.
If we kill twenty a month
We can relax, baby.

Baby, you know well that the best
Governments are those not afraid to kill
Those who make us afraid to go out at night.

Baby, when I kiss your Death Row breasts
I know why I must kill the killers
Who must kill in the dark and die in the light.

You gotta vote right, baby, you gotta vote right.

Modest Enough

Not many men have seen the gods' faces.
I'm proud of the fact
That Jesus and I were on first-names basis
Right from the start.

There was none of Your Reverence, Father,
Right Honourable, Mister, Sir,
Your Grace, Your Lordship, Your Most High,
Your Holiness, Your Majesty, Imperial or

Otherwise. Just plain
Jesus as we tramped the roads
Bulging with sick and dying

Stopping now and again
For what must have been food fit for gods
Though we sometimes ate to the sound of souls crying.

Photograph

I took this natty coloured photograph
Of Lazarus as he emerged from the tomb.
That, in my view, was a miracle and a half.
I doubt if I shall see its like again.

Lazarus had been extinct for several days.
When he was summoned into the light
There was no sign of him awhile, then to our amaze-
ment, looking a bit dazed and underweight,

Lazarus came forth, blinked, gazed around
And said 'I'm dying for a cup of tea
And a slice of Bewley's coarse-brown.' As he drank
And ate, I colour-photographed him, quietly.

Now, when I consider how flesh rots,
I study that photograph. One of my better shots.

The Original Is Lost

'For days after being called back to life I was fine
Apart from a slight dizziness
And a wee pain in my back. Then I began
To miss the comfort of my tomb, tranquil place

Such as might delight a poet in search of solitude
Where the verses can be polished like silver.
I realised I'd lost the death I'd been brooding over
And working towards for decades, in however crude
And blundering a style. I felt this loss most keenly,
So keenly indeed that I placed an advertisement
In the *Lost and Found* section of the *Squirish Mimes*,
"Lost: one death. Small reward offered to finder. Lazarus."

I received a single reply signed *Bargain Basement*.
It said, "I can sell you a second-hand death for 30p.
The original is lost. At a push, this second-hand will suffice."

I didn't answer Bargain Basement. I'll just go on like this.'

Modern Music

'Dying lived down to my lowest expectations.
My death-rattles resembled much modern music
Prompted by a symphony of bloody eructations
And other symptoms of being grievously sick.

Life, I spasm-reflected, is not something I have chosen.
My brain fails, my sight dims, my breathing is farcical,
My balls are frozen.
Thanks be to Christ the tomb is the end of all.

It is in me arse. "Lazarus, come forth!" he said.
Like a schoolboy suffering his first day at school
I came forth, and back to the world of men.

My wife remarked I was looking well after being dead.
I felt, as my friends nudged each other, a bit of a fool
And now I must endure that modern music all over again.'

Cup

I stuck my tongue into the cup when
it was passing round the table and I knew
I drank a heart
because I tasted the blood starting to flow
backwards into the village on a June
afternoon with the old mill grinding its teeth
in the heat and I tasted the blood
in the future among rushes on a roadside

> where Anto Macauley is lying
> shot through the head,
> the right material for
> a fiery ballad

> sung at the wedding of Mary and Joe
> by whole-hearted Danny McGroome
> whose babysitter has fallen asleep

like his three children in their upstairs room
with a bad electrical fault
starting to take effect:
the cup is a burning house
in a screaming wilderness
suddenly childless.

A Religious Occasion

I was there for a purpose, not a lark.
I shall long remember
That Sunday afternoon, one mild September,
Standing with 89,374 Catholics in Croke Park

Hearing the Artane Boys' Band play with verve and spark
The National Anthem and *Faith of Our Fathers*.
The Christian faces of the spectators
Were proof of the hard spiritual work

That goes to make true lovers of sport.
I was part of that crowd, one with the electric feeling
That turns a rigid stranger into an instant brother.

It was, dare I say it, a religious occasion.
The ball was thrown in and those two great teams
Proceeded to kick the shit out of each other.

Nowhere

The camp is nowhere, yet a hundred
Starving stragglers drag in here every day.

Miracles

They may be at the top of your agenda
But they're far down in mine.
Impressed you are by instant healing of lepers,
Rousing the dead, turning water into wine,
Feeding a starving mob on a few scraps,
Making the weak strong, the strong weak,
The crippled walk, the blind see,
Deaf hear, dumb speak –

And to what end? Augustine Clancy,
National Teacher, despairing of my religious knowledge and my
        spelling,
Yanks me out in front of the First Communion class,
Slips down my trousers first, then my fancy
Underpants, lashes my bum till my yelling
Splits the parish. Miracles, my ass!

Before My Time

I'm a terrorist before my time
Conscious of the value of plasticbag blood
The good vibes of creative crime
In the hearts of those turning their backs on God.

There's only one way to treat God:
Walk up to Him and kiss Him.
He appreciates the direct approach.
Mess around, you'll miss Him.

God is a Bomb.
To get the best results, handle carefully,
Time properly, choose a fruitful place
Where you can turn murder into martyrdom.

Follow these instructions or it's likely
Godbomb will blow up in your face.

Who'll clean up the mess then? Bloody disgrace!

Lovers of the Genuine

Lovers of the genuine will warm to Semtex,
My Czechoslovak explosive
Which, packed in a tin can and flung,
Will not encourage targets to live.
    It comes with wooden handle attached,
May be thrown at patrols or dropped from a height
On armoured tanks, using a plastic
Dustbin liner as a parachute.

Semtex is more powerful than disruptive prose
Or detonating verse, so genuine
It must do what it was created to do.
If you're compelled to polite your way through lies
And live the death of average non-man
    Semtex is the line for you,
The only line your heart will know is true.

This New Theory

Historical revisionists are now convinced
'Judas is the only Irishman among the Twelve Apostles'.
Certain local historians are incensed
Yet this new theory has a large following.
Some revisionists say Judas was born in Cork
Others say he was a Dublinman
Others still insist he came from Kerry,
A cute hoor who'd steal the salt out of the holy water.

After all that, I ask myself, who am I?
And then I wonder, does it matter a tinker's curse?
Am I you or Uncle Ted or Carney pilgrimming to Knock?
I know this morning I shall never die
Because like God I'm everywhere although
I think that I may settle in Foxrock.

Back from the Verge

Strong is the urge to go over the top
Like a muddy Cockney, patriotic with murder.
Once again, dear friends, I'm back from the verge
Savouring a shaky sense of order

After sniffing my own sweetfoul dissolution,
About to spend eternity
In a damp rusty horse-drawn caravan
Clattering the roads of Waterford and Tipperary

Condemned never to halt at a roadside bungalow
Opulent, tasteless, yet offering the milk and bread
Without which my anorexic spirit would cease to be.

Back from the verge, outlook varied as a rainbow,
I'm ready for tea and toast, nursing the small talent
God in his odd way concentrated in me.

This Legendary Coastline

This legendary coastline is vulnerable.
Force 9 gales, forty-foot high waves,
Regina Coeli has a crack in her hull,
The drowned are turning in their graves,
The Italian skipper admits
He has 90,000 gallons of my crude on board.
Regina Coeli is drifting towards the rocks.
Good Lord!

Even the Son of Man
Might hesitate to walk on the water tonight.
It is time for the National Emergency Pollution Plan.

Regina Coeli is breaking up. You never can tell
When the sea turns traitor. The oil pukes free.
Begin another slick chapter of hell.

Acid

They sprayed the air with acid
Breathed it like the first promise of love
Heard long ago in the corner of a garden.
They drank non-stop for a week
Sang songs of faith and fatherland
Then from basements and bunkers drew forth
Effigies of me, grotesque and vivid,
'The worst human being ever to walk the earth',

And erected them in public places
Tearing and kicking me
Howling and mocking me
Spitting and jeering me
Screaming for my blood.
I study their faces, not unlike my own.
When I'm in shreds they feel exhausted and good.
I want that mob
To trample me alive
Because every day my interest grows
In the bright lies of perspective,
In the faith of those who think
They constitute the truth in ink.
I'm an effigy, in any case,
Bunting fluttering in the breeze.
Being kicked in the stomach, whipped in the face,
Barbed in various inventive ways
Helps me to see my kind, superior
To me in every way, in an odd light.

It's their words I can't forget.

Words reach me as I'm shredded, words fierce
And simple, knife-edged, obscene, not without wit,
Poetry of course, concise and murderous, you may taste it yet.

Gobblegasp

I happened on the old century, his back
To a blackened wall, eyes jailed in pain.
'What's wrong?' I asked the old hack.
The jacked century gobblegasped, 'My main
Artery is clogged with lies, no air, no air,
Or so my old carcase feels.'
                         'What kind of lies
Make you suffer so?'
                   'Normal' came
The gobblegasp, 'The kind one hears and sees
Everywhere, decent lies, know what I mean?'

'Can I do anything to relieve your pain?'

'Yes, show me a city where the air is clean
And poison doesn't cancerise the rain
And the light's not bruised with hungry crying
And breath is evidence of more than men half-dying.'

'Sorry, old thing' I smiled, 'That dream is dead.
You've been awake too long. It's time for bed.'

The Experiment

I'm not sure where the experiment began.
Some say it was the brainchild of a traffic-cop
Who developed ideas on the nature of man.
Flanagan says it started in a small room behind a breadshop
Where connoisseurs gathered to sample the baker's best
And measure ways in which bread kept them alive
As much, at least, as milk from a mother's breast.
Hitler, who holds all culture springs from people's fear of the grave,
Believes, if I understand him, the experiment started
At an undertaker's party in an Austrian village
Resonant, on that occasion, with music and song.
       Theories of origins vary, yet all are agreed
Somewhere along the line, for reasons hard to grasp,
The experiment went wrong.

V. The chosen few in the heavenly know

Interview

When I was being interviewed for my job as an apostle
I thought Jesus's questions were rather prickly,
Like sitting on thistles.
Yet I answered intelligently

As I could, giving the exact names and numbers
Of persons in the Blessed Trinity,
The birthplace of Joseph the carpenter
And the tricky problem of Mary's virginity.

I answered reasonably well on miracles,
Moses, Abraham, Isaac. I cut
The balls off the false gods. I made a case for whores,

Murderers and sundry criminal misfortunates.
At the end, Jesus nodded. He looked me in the eyes.
'Congrats, Judas' he said, 'The job is yours.'

The Secret

To think that I, the one man for the job,
Easy in my skills as absolute schemer,
Should have helped to birth that murderous mob
Lusting for the blood of its redeemer,

Appals me, or nearly does.
So it continues, this helpless treachery of men
In churches beds governments colleges.
I live again, again

Well-dressed as ever, plausible and good,
A friend of children who will suffer,
Hating fatigue, determined to let it rip

Like bombs hatched in Hitler's blood.
He passes on the secret to his condemners.
He becomes his judges. World explodes. The rest is gossip.

A Potholed Version

Obstacles to conversion are many.
Bringing souls to God is a canny art.
A dedicated lad, I put my heart
Into the job in many's the rough country.

When we were converting Ireland
There was small pleasure, much pain.
Frankly, despite my prayers, fasting, good deeds,
Pilgrimages to bleak centres of penance,
I never grew accustomed to the fuckin' rain.

But worse than that, dear brothers in Christ,
Scattered like mini-abysses throughout the land
Were the Grand Canyon potholes in every road
Gaping like hell's mouths in that boggy sod.

After many broken ankles, cracked shinbones, sprained backs,
We lost
All trust in the inhabitants of the island
And got out fast
To trail elsewhere with the Word of God.

God knows what we left behind.
A potholed version of The Message comes to mind.

So Lost

I will sit here in the dark and name their names
To see if they ever lived in me,
These men I knew and travelled with,
Images in memory

So lost they lack even the power to accuse
Me of what I know I must accuse myself:
Someone was betrayed, that was the bad news,
The rumour multiplied like dust on a shelf,

Multiplied, burying itself under itself, layer
Upon layer, cities, families, griefs, governments, lies,
Until all I have is this darkness calm and deep
Like a parable enlightening the air
Or the same air bearing prayers and sighs
Or an uncontrollable desire to weep

Breaking my eyes
Like tomorrow's traveller
Rocketing through poisoned skies.

Banishment *

These are intelligent cruel eyes
Deciphering me at an ungodly rate
Looking through me as if I were clear water
Devil slurry can never pollute.

       These are the organising hands
Responsible for the long humiliation of my kind.
These are old and new wounds
Inflicted on my body and mind.

This is the anger the insult the imprisonment
The release the need to commit the crime again
The resolve that I shall learn to forget
Judgements of men.
And this is the word that loves in banishment,
Can't be written, is true, who has lived it yet?
It loves criminals, understands rage and hate,
Greed, gluttony, lust, envy, pride
And all the spawning darknesses thriving inside.

Iggy Squelch

Iggy Squelch of Our Cross and Passion University
Did a Ph.D.
On the role of the kiss
In myth and history.

He interviewed me.

Did you kiss him?
Kiss? Yes. There was a kiss.

Did you cause it to happen?
I never kiss anyone
Unless I mean the kiss to mean something.

What was the meaning of that kiss?
The strange thing about kissing is
You never know till afterwards.

You kissed him in the garden?
Yes, yes, I did, I was
Trying to say something,
Whenever I say something
I try to mean what I say,
Unless I mean what I say
I know I don't say what I mean.
Know what I mean?

Were you giving a sign?
I was giving a kiss.

Who was watching?
Whoever was there.

Who was there?
Other people. The whole fuckin' party.

What did they do?
They moved in.

What happened?
Sin.

We continued thus, for hours, if I remember right.
Iggy Squelch was a cute questioner.
There was no escape.
O and I nearly forgot to mention –
Iggy got the whole thing on tape.

Badun

Making a living may unmake a man.
Everywhere I look I see
Victims of responsibility.
They write the lines but the lines don't scan
They write the songs but they're out of tune
With music that is theirs alone;
The dreamed harmony becomes the groan
Of a sick man cursing the moon.

      Not once has the moon given a sign
That it hears the curse of an unmade man
Self-betrayed by doing what's right
But I know a badun walking the line
Between should and won't and must and can.
Irresponsible darkness is the light
By which he plies his trade,
Re-making what making a living had unmade.

Slices

Two handsome waiters wheeled in
This heart-melting cake at the Last Supper.
Just looking at it was enough
To prompt me to commit the sin

Of gluttony. What a cake! It tasted even better
Than it looked. Nearly everyone there
Stared at this heavenly fare
And began to feel fatter.

Peter got a slice, Paul got a slice,
Andrew got a slice, Simon got a slice,
Zebedee got a slice, I was quick to take

My slice, a Bishop dropped in for a slice,
Then a Cardinal, a Pope, infinite priests,
All got slices. Where's the cake? Poor, poor cake!

Unauthorised Version

Would you blame me for thinking the entire
Event was going to come a cropper
When Brendan Behan splattered through the door
Of the room where we were having the Last Supper?

The man was pissed out of his borstal mind,
His trousers at half-mast, blood bubbling his face.
'Where's the fuckin' drink?' he shouted at Jesus.
'Come in, Brendan' Jesus replied, 'Take your place.'

Behan sat down, started swigging the wine
And guzzling the odd lump of bread.
                    After a while
He sang *Tonight is our last night together*
And his own unauthorised version of *Molly Malone*.
                    Jesus smiled.

The Twelve Apostlettes

'How is it?' I asked Jesus, 'You haven't even
A single woman among your twelve apostles?
I mean, aren't you a prejudiced son-of-a-bitch?
Bit of a male chauvinist pig? I'd like to suggest

A dozen women – to be known as the Twelve Apostlettes
Who will constitute an alternative to your men,
Introduce another notion of salvation,
An alternative hell and heaven.

I wish to nominate Sally Noggin, Dolly Mount, Nell Flynn,
Biddy Mulligan, Valerie Valera, myself, Tosser Conner,
Molly Malone, Bonny Bell, Paula Foll, Vinnie Greene

And bearing in mind inevitable sin
As well as necessary concepts of virtue and honour
I nominate, lastly, Mary Magdalene.'

'Thank you,' Jesus smiled (the smile was fleeting)
'I'll bring the matter up at our next meeting.'

A Lambasting

Brendan Behan lambasted me at the Last Supper.
For starters, he told me with a grin
I was a spiritual Jack the Ripper
With a face like a plateful of mortal sin.

Then he said as he dared my eyes
I had the cut of a slithery get
And the innocent Jesus would find in me
What he'd live to regret.

I was, he added, the kind of man
Who gave a divine beauty
To your average rat.

'Finally' he rasped as he downed more wine,
'You're the prison bully and you're hangman-smelly.
And that, Judas, is fuckin' that!'

A Dream of Yellow Rain

If I were a psychologist I might view
What appears to have happened through analysing eyes;
If I were a nuclear scientist I might know
Why certain stars are fiery, icy and wise;

If I were the one I kissed and betrayed
I fancy I'd find it hard to forgive me
    But I am none of these, I am my own
Man, yours, the Good Book's prince of treachery.

Rivers whisper my name, my name smears the sun,
The sun protests, my name rips outcast through space,
Lost planet, shredded effigy, withered bone.
Nameless planets spin to praise his face
And the pained depths of God's unsleeping heart
Harbour a lonely truth: Judas plays his part.
Play me home to the ticking of a clock
Thought of eternity betrayed by time
Where Christ is water and Peter a rock
And yours truly an unruly patron of crime.
I'm still not sure what I did or said
Don't know the meaning of one unblooming thing
Begin in a garden, end with the dead,
Begrudge no man his crust of bread
But doubt your ears when the love-choirs sing.
It happened, I insist it happened, the lads played
Their parts, I wonder did I get them wrong,
What is a prayer, a sin, the magic of money,
A name chosen-created to bear all the blame,
A man-made judgment premature or delayed
Voices whining in beggary or angelised in song,
A world gorged with poisoned milk, poisoned honey?
My sleep tonight is a place of pain.
I am a dream of yellow rain.

Strangers Are Strangers

Decades later I met one of the apostles.
His face had emptied itself of the world's frantic traffic.
He'd abandoned the work nine years earlier
And taken to walking on his own
Through towns and cities in different countries.
He never spoke a word to anyone.
Strangers are strangers and should be left alone, he said.
What difference can my words make?

There's no lessening of pain and humiliation,
Money and money's children are kings,
I knew one moment of knowing, ice in the mind,
I desire not to intrude on anyone ever again,
I live in a world, I know people and things
Die and endure, I wish you, Judas, whatever is good
For you, you are strange to me as loved, lost God.
You were of us, in us, one, though now I hear you are bad,
Bad lad, bad lad, bad lad, bad lad.

The First Time

The first time I kissed The Church
Was at a party in Clonmacnoise.
We were both slightly pissed and lurched
Towards the base of a Celtic Cross
Where the kiss took place. It was a French one,
Sloppy, germful, yet dexterous and long.
'That was refreshing' smiled The Church 'You're a gas man.
Now do sing an Irish song.'

I obliged with *The Rose of Tralee*,
A harmonious rendering of that difficult air
So frequently murdered by drunken women and men.

'That was beautiful' smiled The Church 'I see
No singer in Ireland who can compare
With you. You're pure music, Judas. Kiss me again.'

Guilty But Insane

The Church was hauled up before the Judge
And charged with keeping the people down
Using the Sacraments and the Ten Commandments
As the major instruments of oppression.

81

(The Eleventh Commandment 'Thou shalt not be found out'
The Judge dismissed as a frivolous addition
To the Literature of Hortatory Prohibition
Though he conceded this was the Commandment
Most religiously observed by Irishmen.)

The Church pleaded Not Guilty.
                'I am the people'
The Church said, 'Not merely Popes Bishops Priests
Holy Etceteras. I'm waiting for Christ to come again.'

'Something' the Judge concluded 'Is wrong on a universal
Scale. I should sentence you to two thousand years, at least.
Instead, I find you guilty but insane.'

The Church smiled at The Judge. He blessed himself.

As I Splashed and Swam

The apostles and I were having our daily
Dip in the Forty-Foot for the good of our health.
Peter enjoyed it because it was truly
Electrifying, made him feel like a wealthy

Man. The others liked it too
Even when winter chilled their apostolic balls.
Dalkey! Killiney! Good! Beautiful! True!
And yet, now and then, a strange thing befalls

Even innocent men frolicking in the sea.
To be precise, a strange thing happened to me.
As I splashed and swam I swallowed a lump of shit,

A raw, untreated, solid, calorie-conscious,
Middle-class lump of shit.
It spoiled my day, made me greensick among happy men.

Heavens, shall I ever be unpolluted again?

Under the Table

There was a bomb-scare at the Last Supper.
We were tucking into the bread and wine
When the phone rang in an abrasive manner
And someone said in a Cork accent at th'other end of the line

Dat dere was a big hoor of a bomb in de room, boy.
Unpardonable, I thought. Nothing excused it.
Zebedee found the bomb in a bag under the table.
Jesus defused it.

After that opening shock the evening went well.
Peter got sloshed and showed his old
Tendency to pull rank.

I told him, in the vaults of my mind, to go to hell
And brooded on my tentative efforts to open
An account in a Swiss Bank.

Where Is Little Nell?

You'd never dream, looking at the various paintings,
There was a woman at the Last Supper.
Afterwards, over a few whiskeys, chatting,
She told me it had been her life's ambition
To be present at the final fling because
Male clubs were damaging to men and women alike.
Her name was Little Nell, she gave me pause,
I relished the way she threw the whiskey back,
She was glad the Church was founded on a rock
But feared the rock might sometime become sand
If a woman weren't included in the paintings
Reminding future times of that revealing night
In all its drama and complex trappings.

I examine, in vain, the Great Masters. Where is
Little Nell? Her radiant face? Her sparking yappings?
Her sweeping-away of all male chauvinist shite?
Who ousted Little Nell? Who quenched her cheeky light?
If I could, would I paint her into the scene? I might.

Event

'Please, please address us on the stupidity
Of the Women's Movement, we know you're one
Of the genuine male chauvinist pigs in the city,
Convinced of the natural superiority of man

Over and under woman, we want you to do
A Norman Mailer on those intellectual
Girls who're only aching for it anyway,
We want you to call a cunt a cunt, let it all

Hang out, that'll get them coming, show them
How atrocious their prose is,
We'll guarantee a fee, give you bite and sup,

Just be yourself, grunt at the bitches, you know them,
We've spent months organising this event,
It'll be fun when you fuck it up.'

Fishing

One morning I went out fishing with Peter,
A hot-headed sort, and obstinate
So when he told me to pitch my line in the river
I quickly obeyed. I caught a trout.

'Bravo, Judas!' said Peter, enthusiastic flames
Zipping through his eyes into his beard.
He proceeded to coin affectionate names
For me: Flyboy, Mackerelman, Troutscout, Sharklord.

'Further' he went on, mimicking the master
Whose style of expression is divinely precise,
'I shall make you a fisher of men.'

'Does that mean' I asked, looking through the water,
'I must stick this hook into men's mouths and eyes?'
'O Judas' laughed Peter, 'You're such a clever, foolish man.'

To Work

Suppose I have nothing
But a swift's broken wing
A swift's terrified eye,

                    Is that enough
To keep me strong
When accusers and interpreters
Define my wrong?

Has my enthusiasm cooled?
Am I disappointed because
Enemies who should be cut down
Are not cut down?
Do I smell a false messiah, one who according
To law must be done away with
That yobboes suck authority from myth?
Am I one of many disillusioned men,
One of many, yet the only one
To do what must be done?
Should not this power proclaim itself,
                    arise and sing
To hearten people whose hearts are low?
Must noble blood be spilled to breed a cosmic lie?
Will yuppies thrive because one knew how to die?
Accusers, interpreters, to work, for I
          Have a swift's broken wing,
A swift's terrified eye.

Your Wan's Answer *

If Bishops could
Get pregnant
Abortion would
Be a sacrament

A Minor Rôle

I could have organised the ship from stem to stern,
Sidestepped the crucifying mess.
Had they listened, I'd have made them learn
Ways to bridle chaos.

I could make a Buddhist and a Hindu chat together
Discussing Protestant and Catholic views
On the changing state of atheistical weather.
I could make the Arabs love the Jews.

Instead, my organising genius was ignored,
I played a different part in that vast
Redemptive plan,

Mere cheeky kisser of my prayerful Lord.
A minor rôle, you'd say. Why must
Gods always pick the wrong man?

The Dark Night of the Hole

I was cycling home from a disco in Nazareth
Under the luminous vacuity of a harvest moon
Which tempted me for a moment to take my eyes
Off the road, o giddy-treacherous man!

Failing to spot the warning blink
Of the local Corporation lamp
I cycled straight into a hole, sink-
ing without trace, apart from the damned

Screams I somehow hurled at the moon
Like a mob's insults at a crucifixion.
My bike was in smithereens. So was I
In that profound hole, stinkydeep like my mind

Which proceeded to release imbeciles and demons
To tell me Irish/Jewish jokes through all eternity.
Workers found me in the morning. I'm glad I was found.

The dark night of the hole returns now and then
Like the bad jokes told and relished by passing men.
Who the hell makes up these jokes? Did you hear this one...?

Whatever I Am

Whenever I run into the other apostles nowadays
They glance the other way.
Peter is the only one to halt for a moment
Turn on me his fierce eye
As if he's going to unleash one
Of those enraged tirades I find so endearing
But even Peter manages to keep the lid on.

I'm out in the cold, all on my ownio.

Theological types argue I'm lost
My psychological friends speak sadly of alienation
Whatever I am, it's not nice.

How could it be? My brain is packed in frost
My blood, a poisoned tributary of the Shannon
My heart, a regular thump of ice

Though I saw miracles once, miracles, you realise.

Laureate

For ages the apostles toiling in silence
Kept no chronicle of their affairs
Content to spend their days working for love
Seeking no praise.

Then one said 'Judas, you have a way with words,
Write a poem, a song
To celebrate the fortitude of these good men
Who've laboured long.

Be our poet Laureate!
In verse that trips, tinkles, resounds,
Remind the crass world that we are here.
We'll give you silver and beer.

Sing of Herod's birthday, Hitler's enterprise,
The Pope's decision to dress in white
When black despair envelops the hearts of men
To left and right.'

I accepted the offer. I wrote a verse praising
TIME MAGAZINE for choosing Hitler
1938 Man Of The Year.
Everyone said my poem was amazing.
I deserved my silver and beer.

Beer and silver, silver and beer —
I still compose the occasional celebratory titbit
Lacking in passion, perhaps, but with my special tricky skill.
I make startling use of the hortatory cliché —
Honour thy father, Love thy neighbour, Thou shalt not kill.

I do not expect my verse to be collected,
Enough for me the plaudits of the moment.

Ignoring slanderous chit-chat, envious jeer,
I celebrate the official apostles
In my own style, modest and transient
Amid beer and silver, silver and beer.

The Job

Why didn't I get the job? The thought
Is something of an obsession.
If I'd been appointed I'd have changed
The image of the Apostolic Succession.

With my special talent who knows
What might have happened?
Would the Church be facing
Its present state of spiritual collapse?

Peter was first choice.
Judas the traitor, Peter the rock:
Perish the labels; we soldiered together once.
Peter was able-bodied, quick-tempered, strong-voiced,
Good-hearted. But did he do the trick?
Or is the rock self-smashed into smithereens?
Why do the most living hearts
Attract the deadest has-beens?
How did that passionate adventure
Become a bad theological lecture?
How did the agony of loving eyes
Become a sordid political enterprise?
Although my soul is helplessly adrift
I have a few questions left.
There'll be no answers till the polished men
Get the smell of blood from the hill again.

The Question

Whenever I see the apostles getting bored
Or about to grow
Pissed-off with the responsibility placed on them by the Lord
I ask the question 'Who killed Marilyn Monroe?'

Two weeks before she died she sang 'Don't be
Uptight on a Saturday night' over the phone
To John F. Kennedy on his birthday.
Stilled is that voice. Dead naked alone

The ravishing innocent was found in her bed.
Who did it? The Mafia? The Kennedys? The CIA?
The Pope? The UDF? The Anti-Abortion Society of Crossmaglen?

Two thousand years have fled since this matter came to a head.
It dies away for decades. Then, prompted by moralists like me,
It surfaces. We talk. The apostles sparkle like lovers born again.

VI. You

If I, If You

If I had not betrayed you
How would you have accomplished the miracle
In the unspeakable cities
Where children develop a killing style

Early? Would men have been so brave
Or women so given up to your memory?
Who would have dreamed it possible to save
Vanishing humanity from the hard-earned grave?

    And if you had not betrayed me
How could I ever have begun to know
The sad heart of man? How could I,
Watching seas of greed lick the shores of the
World and vanity all the human show,
Have found the courage to die?

If we swapped questions, o my brother,
Would we know why we betrayed each other?

Voice

The voice began, a scrape of nails over flesh,
Became the sound of rutting badgers, then
Was that drunk dung-faced fire-eyed cursing foul-
Smelling man who staggered to the frying-pan
On the Stanley range, lifted the sausages,
Stuffed them into his gob,
Savaged the brown loaf, looked at me,
Closed his eyes, moaned, started to sob
But checked himself. What he said next
I did not understand at the time. Nor do I now.
It's his voice I remember. For thirty years

I forgot all, the curses, remorse, bewilderment,
Blind oaths of revenge. Last night, the voice cut me
In two. I wanted to kill it, but froze in fear.
I don't know what it said but my heart
Cringed, a beaten dog. I got the long knife
And waited. Stab the voice, I thought, stab the curse.
Even as I knew it didn't exist, it grew worse,
I was split and maddened by what
Was not,
Growing more vile and foul in me. I had to kill it, kill
Nothing. It's gone, it raves and threatens still.
Did you arrange this? Am I accomplishing your will?
Are you nothing too? Nothing? Pretending to be all?

A Casual Masterpiece

I am sitting here in my silence
Listening to your silence
Away from the streets of poison
And the cocksure minds
Blackleathering it across the pages.
I know now I can never be lost enough
In the silence, the only gift to survive the rages
And pains of a heart waiting to trip over love
In this tedious crazy place
That hates itself more than Hitler the Jews
And is better equipped to destroy
A glimpse of heaven in a turning-away face,
A casual masterpiece
Of this winter afternoon's eruptive joy.

A Sweet Jig

I sat under a palm-tree watching the sun
Doing a sweet jig on the water
And thought for all I was worth
(Not much) about the matter:

91

I imagined you were at my side
Listening with that patience unknown to other men.
'I did it' I said, 'Not from greed, vanity or pride
But because I believed it was the right plan.

May I ask did you suspect me from the start?
Did you know everything living in my mind?
Did you smile to mine the pits in my heart?
Was I a bright man? Or was I stupid and blind?'

We sat under the palm tree, I talking, you listening.
I waited. You looked at me, through me, said nothing.

Lonelier

Something lonelier far than you or me...

Down here
In the heart's hell, the crumbling skin,
The trembling hand,

There are small moments when all I care to do
Is praise the loneliness
I cannot understand.

A Bird

I am haunted by a name.
If I battered my head against a wall
The blood would form into the name's letters at my feet,
If I prayed to a god who eats men's brains
To stimulate his drowsy intelligence
He'd send the name in the wind and rain
Like a never-before-heard bird out of the sun,
A bird whose bones are made from the longings of the dead,
A bird with one song

Repeated with a keen, unsatisfied passion
Claiming my heart and my head
   and far beyond
Whatever I think I know of right and wrong.

I Was There

If, at any time in the future,
You enter this garden, drunk
Out of your puny mind,
And submit another man
To the evil scrutiny
Of your inquisitional glare,
Try not to drown the poor creature
In the foul boghole of your breath.
Last time you reeked in, I was there.

Child of the Sword

I dreamed we were waiting for a train
To go where there was a chance to be happy.
Somebody stabbed somebody up the line,
I ran to the victim, his neck was bloody.

There beside him lay Saint Bridget's Peace Cross.
It said, 'One day, a beggar called to her
Asking for alms. Bridget looked in the man's eyes
And seeing whatever she saw there

Gave him her father's sword. Today, right here,
A child of that sword stabbed a man in the neck,
He's quiet in his blood now, tonight he'll be raving,

Tomorrow a corpse.'

           The Cross is polluted air,
The train roars goodbye at my back,
You lean from a window, smiling, waving.

The Hell of an Effort

If you haven't been there, you don't know it.
If you have, you don't speak of it.
Isn't it fierce weather for the time o' year?
Thanks be to Jesus Flanagan isn't here.

A day at a time, that's how you manage.
You know you'll never undo the damage
You did to Kitty, Pete and Albert Lou.
Fact is you've made them sicker than you.

Two hotels, a family, part of your brain,
The whole kaboosh flushed down the drain,
The hell of an effort is needed now
Keep telling yourself that you know how
To live with demons living in your ear
And thanks be to Jesus Flanagan isn't here.

Where You Come From

Hell is not where you go to, it's where you come from.
You come from here, this place, this black hour.
It's bad here at the moment
With a lunatic in power
Children dying off like decency
Flogging torture starvation mockery
Black magic witchcraft poisoning of wells
The air packed with agonised cries
Our women vanishing leaving no traces
Our city besieged with a new disease
Old devils wearing new faces

And all the bad out there thriving here at your side.

But don't worry, I have keys
To unlock your prison, compensation awaits
You, heaven, I tell you that, when have I ever lied?

The Madness of Football

Beautiful country, driven-out people –
Yakuntya, yahoorya, yabollocksya,
And the boys and the girls studying
For jobs in another country:
                Beautiful country, driven-out people –
I remember Mad Sweeney,
District Inspector Sweeney, to be exact,
Issuing guns in the Phoenix Park
And telling the RIC men
To open fire on the crowds in Croke Park.
Was there a Final feeling that Sunday
Or a totally different kind of sport,
A breakthrough in virile craft and art?
The papers forecast a battle royal.
I stewed in the crowd, I saw men fall.
Beautiful country, driven-out people –
I'm shot through with the madness of football.
Run, hit, kick, score, win. Win. That's all.

Teabags

I too have seen God in teabags, heard
Him lisping in the ticking of my clock
Tocking Sinai interpretations of the Word
Intended to improve my luck

                but I end up
Smelling my neighbours in church shop theatre
Damp creatures preparing for the long drop
From mortgages and babies and those peculiar
Forms of concern that cause this pimpled youngster
To spittle me in the street with
'I hate the bastard! I hate my bloody father,
Trying to live my life for me, shape me
Into his own fascist narcissistic middle-aged myth.
What can you say to me? What can you do for me?
This is bad, Judas. This is really bad!'

I'm perplexed-profound. 'Teabags' I mutter 'Study each feature
Of teabags. Be mystical. You'll understand your dad.
Place teabag in cup, pour boiling water, let it steep,
Extract teabag, throw it away, then drink, my son,
        drink deep of love and hope.'

Deep

Now and then throughout my career, let me
Call it career, I've tried in my grisly solitude
To open a dialogue with God.
'Good morning, God' I say, 'And how are things with you today?'

Silence. I wait a while before pursuing the matter
Then, hoping a cultural topic might prompt a reply,
Murmur, 'I'm getting interested in Nazareth folklore,
I bet you have fond memories of that, eh?'

Devil a word. But I don't give up easily.
I probe. 'Are you happy with the way things have turned out?
Does your favourite creature love the good, the beautiful, the true?'

Dumber than the dead. Silence deep as eternity.
I used to be disappointed but now that I think of it
If I'd made the world I'd keep my mouth shut too.
Especially if I'd made me, I imagine
Dialogue with me would not be my prime concern.

Reeling *

Who would have dreamed
Seeing you reeling
The streets of Dublin
Hurting yourself
As if you were the only man
You never could forgive

That your words would tell
Young men and women
How to live?

I might have dreamed it
If I'd fallen asleep
But I'm a sly, vigilant,
Wideawake creep.

Bed

They wrote me down! The watchers wrote me down!
What sneaking watcher had the gall to write me down?
There are more versions of me than there are judging men.
When the master spoke, he said he was one,
Or three-in-one, or one-in-three, some such drivel.
A few who use words speak heart and soul,
Speak the blood's black skies as far as they're able.
Eat soulwords, heartwords, bloodwords. Or go to the devil.
The devil may not have you, of course, he's very pernickety
About those he's willing to use his words on.
He told me he once spent seven eternities,
Including an eternity chez God, struggling to find his own
Voice. When he did, it surprised even himself
With its infinite range of infernal effect.
His accent is bland, posh, with the occasional
Descent into crude if colourful peasant dialect.
He loathes vulgarity, he suspects it's good for the soul,
He has a liking for Sanskrit and official forms
Of Irish, he gives the nod to Anglo-Saxon's rutting edge,
Milton is his favourite poet, he thinks the Bible is crap,
Forbids his kids to read it, might keep them free from harm
And harm teaches kids the nature of the storm.
Such is the devil's word-mastery, he's turned hell into a college
Where choice language is really on the map.
        The Map of Ireland is what girls making beds in hotels
Dub semen-stains of sleepers on the sheets.
I leave it to you to imagine who makes the devils' beds in hell
And what they call the sheetstains of the devilsleep,
If sleep there be. Who lies in a devil's bed?

97

Who lies in yours? In yours? Lies, lies, lies,
Who knows the cosy hole where Cain was chosen to be bad?
What was your hot spawning-spot? Or mine?
I flatter myself, a castellated Victorian double-poster,
I'm just joking, y'know, I must, and yet I speculate
(You must too) on the warmth of that populating stink.
Every cretin among us has to come from somewhere,
Trouble starts in bleedin' bed, some usual stupo night,
In the beginning was the word and the word was – well, what do
        you think?
Think! Think until you are a pain-thorned head.
What then? Your favourite pills. Fall into bed.

Whatever You Want

Not to the living but to the dead do I grant sincerity.
I listen closely to those who have nothing to say.
Throw yourself on the bed, darling, weep fiercely
And between vast heart-racking sobs tell
Why priceless Simon went away.
My floor is covered with tears and snot
I'm being swept into your lachrymose hell
Where sincere devils cry in their chains and rot
And wish me well.

Give me that old cold-hearted loonypuss moon
Shining on its icy own
Hanging there to charm aspiring eyes
Being whatever you want it to be:

Clownmug, angel's harp, last loverword,
Heaven's magnetic turd,
Yellow bucket full of human lies.
Is the yellow bucket sincere? Do you think it tries?
Or are you deaf and dumb
And caged in your own sighs?

In the Wings

Many died that I might exist.
Either that or they were rough drafts
For me, the finished poem you read in your lost
Youth one day you saw a hawk culling sparrows.
Only your eyes saw this. Otherwise, it didn't exist.
You kept it to yourself, a small
Fierce parable of the order you believed in.
Let others call it murder. You knew it was mercy.

So victims arrange themselves into neat rows
To accommodate their executioners. In the wings,
Moralists buzz like flies over shite,
You are coming into being, nothing can stop you,
One witness complains, another sneers, another sings
Of the role you play in the birth of the immortal light.

Pure Wonder *

When I leaned into the kiss
Did he return it, more or less?
Was that the moment I knew release
From all thoughts sick and treacherous?

doorway

why, in that moment
of heart's darkness, of
severance without end,
did you turn to me
in the freezing doorway,
smile and say 'I'll always
be your friend'?

VII. High on silver

The Bribe

So much, so little, no more, that's it, what is it?
What do you want for that?
Do you think you can buy me for that?
All of me? My heart? Mind? Body? Soul?

Why do you smile when you make the offer?
Do you know something about me I don't know?
Are you so confident I'll take the bait?
The bribe? That's what it is, isn't it? The bribe?

And I am to change the world for that!
And you'll get what you want and so will I
And this is the moment we both know something true.

Wipe that smile off your face, you pious respectable rat,
Someone who can't be bought is about to die.
Give me the money, here's what I'm going to do.

Little Jewel

In that nasty Wall Street crash
I lost fifteen of my thirty pieces of silver.
My heart will not recover those missed beats
Nor my spine forget the shiver
Twanging my brain for days.
Did I allow the disaster to throw me?
No. I counted the fifteen pieces that remained
And bought six bottles of Black Bush whiskey.

I said to myself, silver is only silver
And there's more where the thirty pieces came from.
That high-priest thought helped me to survive.

The old question, what is money? is fascinating as ever.
The fact that silver is inseparable from my name
Is a little jewel that makes me glad I'm alive.
Let planets crash and smash, I hoard my shame
As a miser hoards every shilling.
When the moment comes to invest, I'll make a killing.

Circulating Bags

Whenever I go to Mass
I am impressed by the sound of money
Dropping into circulating bags
Handled by the most faithful of the faithful.

And I think of that angry afternoon
When the dreamer, having released the doves from their cages
Fell into one of his rare, scattering rages
And booted the moneymen

Out of the temple into the street.
Then I see the necessity for cash
And wonder would heaven, or what seems
Like heaven, endure without it?
I once cashed a cheque in the Bank of the Holy Spirit,
I know what it means to buy and sell dreams
And cannot say, therefore, who will inherit
The earth or any part of it.
Circulating bags suggest money is the heart of it.

Wallet *

Is it the world? Is it me?
Every street I walk I see
Men and women
Made of money.

Has anybody cried
Because the world is a wallet

And we're all tucked up inside?

Wisdom *

This was Arab Africa.
I was seeking wisdom
With that calm fanatical devotion
I've known now and then in dream.
I crossed bridge after bridge
Scoured town after dirty town
In vain. Then the sand rose
And lashed me up and down
Territories without a name.
I conquered the sand
Or simply outwalked it.

        I found the man
At last, the dream one. I asked for wisdom.

'Beware', he said, 'What you clasp in your hand.
You're fond of silver, Judas. Too fond.
Forget the silver, son.'

I said nothing. Nodded my thanks. Walked on.
Silver stretched from me to the horizon.

from Thirty Pieces of Silver

2

I was lost in earth-loosening rain,
Slipped underground.
     Passers-by trample on treasure.
     Will I ever be found?

3

Sitting at the driver's wheel, he questions her
Standing sexy-perfect by the red Vauxhall.
He gives me to her, she slips me into her purse
From which dark sanctuary I can hear him
Fucking her against the hospital wall.
In the distance, an ambulance brays,
A dog begins to howl. The man is getting small,
Smaller and (o pricey night!) smaller again.
Fulfilment shrivels the best of men.
I lie in the darkness, the price of their pain.

5

Eve Lynch stands at the door of her pub,
Her last customer leaves, blind with bliss.
She mutters, watching him reek into the night,
'I have your money, handsome, and you have your piss.'

11

I made the rifle available to the boy.
Newspapers christen him a terrorist.
When he has killed three men and a woman
He'll have earned the bosses' trust.
He'll be shot dead one September evening
Having dinner in a hotel in another town.
The newspapers will speculate for a day or two.
Then the killers will admit the killing over the phone.
Communication thrives; I flourish; some hopes begin to sink.
What would happen if the guns began to think?

13

A tourist drops me into a tinker's cap
On a sleety bridge. Poverty! Poverty!
The tinker hoists his arse from the ancient blanket
And hobbles off for a hot whiskey.

14

I have watched you grow to love me
In the sick prison where I made you free.
I am the way the truth and the life.
No one cometh to the Manager but by me.

16

I built a university,
Dedicated it to learning's fastidious god.
There, I said to a young man who saw through books,
Is where the best things are scrupulously misunderstood.

18

I'm a priceless trinket
Blood of war
Goodbargain bad Spanish wine
        in your local supermarket
Slave-labour
Reason for Junkie Jordan to drown or not drown
Stinking digs in Camden Town.

22

The old saint's body turns ecstatically sick
When he sees heaven flowing
From the eye of the bright boy's prick.
Though my nature resists total knowing
My interest is growing all the time
At home in law, at home in crime.
With me, without me, hearts learn to quake.
I'm the best teacher of heaven and sex the world has known.
Money talks, they say. Wrong. I'm silent, I don't even
Have a mind of my own. All the other minds
Pour into my no-mind. Some will surface, many drown.

My no-mind knows heaven is a night on the town
With gods and goddesses letting their hair down.
The bright boy is beginning to know his price.
The old saint is breaking the holy ice.

25

I vanish into the hole
Wander lucrative and lost
Until I come to rest on Society Hill,
Philadelphia. In a pseudo-Georgian mansion
I am gold.
This evening at dinner, glittering amid chat,
I decorate a beautiful throat.
I shine for her, being part of her plan.
Ted Weiner's eyes caress me a moment,
Return to his duck.
I like the feel of her neck, sound of her heart beating,
Velvet pulse of her intent.
Out of the hole I came, and may return,
Love's instrument.
When her fingers touch me, I am all astonishment.

26

Little poem is all but written.
What to do with the singing thing
That already is assuming the look of a lived-in
Dutiful shabbypolished old shoe?
Mr Editor, how much do you pay
For a moment of durable insight
Into this perishing day?
Enough for last month's fire? Next month's light?
What price a modest spot, a garden flat
On a hillock in the shade of Parnassus
    With hot
    And cold
And ever-expanding realms of gold?
    God bless us!
Is that all? Finito? Caput? Nothing more?
    Send the poor poem
    To a Stray Dogs' Home

Where it can snore away its days
Rousing itself odd times to gnaw an old bone
Shaped like someone's notion of inspiration.

29

I have not chronicled the wars fought for me,
       Rarely in my name.
I sponsor conferences on the nature of happiness
       When I have buried the young men
Who died to order, by mistake.
I purify the water sipped by arthritic professors
In the rebuilt hotel by the fabricated lake.
I publish the precise, inane theories that lead nowhere
       Or back to themselves, nowhere.
I nourish the gutsy ambitions of the escapees
And hear their prayers for a renovating month in Greece
Along with me, away from me, away from the stones
       Over the heads of the young men
       Resting and rotting in peace,
Pennies fallen from their eyes, flesh from their bones.
I turn young men into innocent skeletons.

30

Caught!
You cannot hold.
A slot, thank God, a slot.
I fit, copper is silver is gold,
You empty yourself into thankGod the sea,
       The sea
       Filthy and free.
Your flesh blood bones could disintegrate and vanish like that
       But you pick yourself up
       Brace yourself
Like sad Adam equipped only
With the consciousness of his mistake
And speculate into the light, looking for me
       Using my language with such well-coined skill
It stamps your heart, and lives there, as poetry never will.

Limits

Stepping outside limits has always been
A remarkable feature of my character
Though at times I fear I'm a cautious knacker.
Given the prevalence of greed among men
I might have asked for three thousand pieces of silver
But I stepped beyond the limits of greed
By limiting myself. I sometimes see, as in a trance,
Paradox is my natural element, my soul needs
The stimulus of an intricate metaphysical dance
Though my assassin's patience permits me to see
Good fortune is a quickly taken chance.

With my thirty pieces I am content to be
A modest investor in the stock market.
A small profit affords me maximum delight
A shy gesture suggests cosmic mystery
A timely silence bristles with killing wit
And limits, properly used, beget the infinite.

Some Creature

The night I got Businessman of the Year Award
I spoke with charm and some rhetorical skill
On why one must be always on one's guard,
How imagination and will
Should guide the hand turning the wheel of money.
I told three judasjokes, they went down well.
One, in particular, was queer but funny
As hell. This was one joke I had to sell.
They bought it, beaming, told it to their wives
Who laughed amid cosmetic blushes.
They bought it too, big deal, I do not lie.

Later, strolling by dark rebellious waves,
I heard some creature, in the chill reaches
Of the night, emit a piteous, heart-scalding cry.

107

Head

This greedy head belongs to the landlord
Of the Last Supper Inn:

He's a long, thin slieveen of a mick
From somewhere in Leitrim,
He owns houses from Nazareth to Donegal,
He's a moneylender, a bailiff,
An auctioneer committed to smiling:

Goes to mass every morning
Pays Christmas and Easter dues
Picks wives and husbands for his daughters and sons.

When a Bishop dies he slides into mourning
Profitable tears stockexchange his eyes
Which, could you see them, are soft as stones.

Number One

The Pinstripe Pig, good friend, much given
To farting in public and private
Knows his flatulence is perfume from heaven.
He will sit

For long, meditative hours
Loving the smell of his own farts
Though other humans may feel sick.
Inspired by love of that heavenly smell

Pinstripe decides to preserve the music,
Bowls off in his Rolls to his Personal Studio
Records his farts for several days
Edits that music till the work is done,

The record made. Light of his eyes rivals the sun.
Pinstripe enjoys a cult following now
In Russia Asia The Ganges The Himalayas.
Here in the West, he's Number One.

That Pinstripe Air

The Pinstripe Pig loves works of art
Pays gigantic sums to adorn his office.
Gigantic sums? Squeaky financial farts
From that art-loving orifice.

Pinstripe loves Victorian scenes,
Family gatherings, Sunday afternoons,
Garden frolics, Fathers advising sons,
Sensitive clouds touching Autumn moons.

How oft have I spied him there
Alone
Contemplating pictures with that Pinstripe air

Well-known to ladies rich and debonair,
Well-known to lovers
Of art and cash, everywhere.

Money in Love

My good friend, the Pinstripe Pig, says
There's money in love
Especially in shining teenage eyes.
Pinstripe's mind, all bonny-bladed edge,
Hires me to write songs
That shiver their little fannies
While they pour out tears and screams
And tidal monies.

Pinstripe sits in his office all day
Breaking record after record.
'Thanks be to God' he sighs 'for the fucking young,
The fucking young.'
                    Child, if you're lucky,
Pinstripe will blow you a kiss, he's music-lord
Thrilling your days with love's old sweet song.

Listen to Pinstripe, child, and you can't go wrong.

Experiment

I have been short of silver in my time.

Strolling dolefully along High Street, Killarney,
I met an Englishman with a catchy name.
He asked me if I'd like to make some money.

Soon to a London clinic we were bound.
Packed with healthy types (but broke) the place was big
And opulent. Imagine my surprise when I found
I was chosen as a human guinea pig.

I have no bone to pluck with radioactivity
But for years following my experiment
I was sudden fits, blackouts, migraine.

The things a hard-up man will do for money!
I have a sense of self-betrayal. Be assured I shan't
Endanger my health if I'm stuck for cash again

For in my wisdom now I know a pig is not a man
Although (let me whisper this to you)
The reverse is sometimes true.

Without Love or Colour *

Lecherous wretches of the dream survive
While you and I can stay alive.
We have been down in places where
There's no colour in a girl's hair

Only a sense of evil in
The purposeful eyes of men,
A world without love or colour.
Another day, another dollar.

Not Rich

I am not a rich man and yet I was hauled up
Before the Chief Tax Commissioner whose rigour
Has robbed many a man of bite and sup
Because I failed to declare my thirty pieces of silver.

I found the Commissioner's questions rather unnerving
And yet I answered succinctly as I could:
How did you earn this not inconsiderable sum, sir?
Kissing.
And who, may I enquire, did you manage to kiss?
God.
I see.
I knew you'd see, your Honour.
Are your expenses heavy?
Like a cross.
Will they grow heavier?
Yes, forever on the increase.
Do you intend to make more silver out of kissing?
No, your Honour, as a business it's a dead loss.
You're an honest man, Judas. Live tax-free. Go in peace.

Pawn

Determined, from the start, to be nobody's fool
I launched into my scrutiny of money with the kind
Of disciplined fury that frightens a weaker mind,
Continued my research at Harvard Business School

Where Yankee genius burned me hot under the collar.
I steadied my nerves sufficiently
To produce my globally-applauded study
On the Origins and Development of the Dollar.

Money is amazing when you come to think of it.
It absorbed me as I sipped Common Room Sherry
And drank the sun on my favourite New England lawn.

111

My academic intensity deepened. Yet when I visited
The High Priest, I heard him muttering to himself:
'Here comes a king-sized pawn.'

Brother James

Short of cash one morning
Feeling spiritually out of breath
I raised my drooping heart by purchasing
James Joyce's death-mask at an auction in Nazareth

For forty pence.
I took it to my Traitor's Pad
And studied it for hours.
No trace there of magical poetic powers.
James Aloysius Joyce looked sad,

Puzzled, constipated, waxed, hungover, blind,
Exiled, cunning, silent as the Liffeybed.
Has it, I whispered to the death-mask, come to this?

It has, you know it has, you prick, the mask replied,
You'd feel the same if you were auctioned dead.
O brother James, I sobbed, and gave the mask a kiss.

If I'd a Heart

I sit appalled at savage yuppie inanity
And shiny moneyboys snaking into power,
I smile as converts to Judasanity
Increase in numbers hour by hour.
Welcome, my daughters! Welcome, my sons!
Welcome, my aspiring hearts!
I cock my ear to hear your orisons
But can't steer clear of your neurotic farts.

Not shrinking from the stink, I think of you
And gazing on your faces now my mind
Transforms my thirty pieces into a special drink.

I pour this in a silver cup, offer it to
You to taste. You taste. How do you find
It? Good? Good. If I'd a heart, I think that it might sink.

Thank You, Silver

It was good to get the silver in my hand.
When the priest gave me the pieces I put them
Into my purse and went home.
I drank several glasses of wine, my mind
Excited as it always was when
I found something comprehensible and real,
Something I could see was beautiful
And untainted by men.

O radiant and resonant silver, I see you now
As once I saw the light of faith at my window,
The light of love at my door,
The light of hope on a dirty worker's brow.

In years to come, people will debase you,
Murder your light with their acquiring eyes
Forgetting what you were created for,
Not to pass from hand to hand
But to startle darkness underground,
Caged music there, truly, purely there,
To hear if you were lost enough to hear.
I hear it everywhere. Thank you, silver.

VIII. All the same in the dark

For Lack of Love

If somebody had loved me then
Kissed me in the street
Would I have done what I have done?
For lack of love a man will up and out

And maim or kill;
For lack of love he'll poison the sea
And sky, cripple the innocent trees;
For lack of love a man won't recognise

Whoever wants to bless and cherish him,
Bring gifts to his door, kind words
To his heart, open that heart when it closes

Like a purpose concentrating to a bullet
Or a knife plunged into a conversation.
For lack of love a man is blighted more than he supposes.

Outside, in the leafy pathway

Just then I knew that loneliness
Was the truedeep thing in my life
(But nothing I'd write home about)
And as I turned away from the faces
Full of untold stories
I knew that I must laugh or die.
I opened my jaws, I laughed and laughed
Till the tears ran down my spirit
And the black rain of memory and misfortune
Was bearable, bearable. I had no need to ask
Where are you now, you passionate
People of dust and love, where are you now
You dreamers chancers drinkers killers thieves clowns?

I stood alone in the black rain and laughed
At what had happened, had still to happen.
Something that had been imprisoned forever
Began to open.
Something that had never dared listen to love
Began to listen.

This Man

There is this man I meet who spittles me stories of sex
As if it were going out of passion.
He's a small badger-headed gobshite with mean eyes
And a hideous jollity in his voice.
I would like to slice him into grim little pieces
And distribute these pieces to dogs
Prowling in ravenous packs both night and day
Through our valium suburbs.

That's what I would like to do. Instead, of course,
I swallow like a disciple his lewd gospel.
Sometimes I enjoy it, sometimes I do not

Because I have this vision of the world as a man
With mean eyes and a hideous jollity in his voice.
I smell his heart, his guts, I absorb his rot.

In spite of that, on certain days I see
This odious contraption is preferable to me.

A Livin' *

            'Five women he has workin'
For him up around Merrion Square,
Five culchie bitches, good at the game,
Every woman a hard grafter, great stayer,
Right perfume in the hair.

When they come back to him every night
He has two heavies to give 'em
A bit of a goin'-over.

That's what they like, he says,
If you don't hit 'em they don't work.

He's a bad bastard, bad an' blunt.
Makes a livin' outa culchie cunt.'

War

'And did you see the Coolun
       Taking a stroll
              For the good of her health?'

'I did, she chose a street
With four lights on one side, none on the other,
Deserted except for a drunk
Muttering as he pissed, pissing as he muttered.

       And she took
A deodorant spray, penknife, scissors, iron bar
Because she knows that going for a walk
In that place at that time of night
       Is going to war.

Every night the Coolun goes to war.
Why not stay at home? What's she trying to find?
       Beautiful body, frightened mind,
Menacing shadows, abuse spat from the dark,
       Footsteps from behind.'

The Coolun

'And did you see the Coolun
Going down the road?'

'I did, she was going into a field
To have a baby all on her own
And there was a statue of Mary
The Virgin Mother of God
Staring down on the Coolun
Twisting in her blood

And then the Coolun died in the field
And her child died at her side
And the grass was the colour of wrong
O the Coolun was immature
And we whispered together and lied
How we wanted her to belong.'

She Muttered

'And when did you last see the Coolun?'

   'About ten days ago.
Her belly was out like a pup's
   And she was going

To England for an abortion.
   She hadn't combed her hair
And she was in a bit of a quandary
   Looking for the fare.

And the Coolun doesn't like sailing
But here was a boat she had to take
To lose the child she had to lose.

She had sad eyes but crying had no meaning,
She muttered something about a random fuck
   And the right to choose.'

She Knows the Smell

'And did you see the Coolun lately?'

'I did. She's on the dole
And trying to stop a thousand drunken Irishmen
Getting up her hole.'

'And is she still the same bright girl,
The shining one, heart's pulse, a joy to greet?'

'As a matter of fact, the Coolun is finding it
Hard to make ends meet
On twenty-nine quid a week.'

'But is she not made of riches
Beyond the dreams of men living and dead?'

'What the Coolun is made of, I dare not speak.
I only know, in this land of bastards and bitches,
She knows the smell of many a bed.'

A Brainy Lady

The lady is a scented wench who would
Intellectualise a simple fuck,
Analyse my sperm, I declare to God.
Here in my modest chalet at the edge
Of the Dead Sea, she throws me a brainy look
And suggests a study of my envious heart.
Our precarious relationship may come unstuck
If I don't comply with her analytic art.
I ponder, moodbrood, philosophyfart,
Suggest with Aristotelian cop-on
The mind betrays what it analyses overmuch.

She analyses this. I wait, sensitively hurt,
Misunderstood by a brilliant woman.
She relents. We fuck. She analyses such and such....

Topping an Egg

'She was one of these quiet Irish girls,
You'd swear butter wouldn't melt in her mouth
Or in any other imaginable orifice
With her hands guarding her legs
And her legs protecting each other

But Jesus in heaven when she started to come
I thought she was going to bite lumps
Out o' me. That same tame little girl

Was a fuckin' maniac, she tore strips
Outa my back, she gartered my hands,
The blood of her cunt stamped my left leg.

Next morning, her chaste lips
Expressed exquisite bafflement at the problem
Of which end she was expected to top her egg.'

Little Budd

There were twenty nuns in the darkened room.
Sister Budd, like all the others, took down her pants
And whipped her bottom.
Swish! Swish! flicked the whips. The women panted

And thought of God.
That night, in bed, Sister Budd lay on her back.
There were bruises, cuts, a little blood.
She crossed her hands on her breasts and shook
With pleasure at the thought-touch.
If she died tonight she could be lifted
Straight into the coffin.

Years later, married, her husband loved to watch
Her in that position. 'Budd' he whispered, 'Little Budd,
Lights on, close your eyes, open your legs, I'm fuckin' laughin'.'

Little Budd giggled: 'Where would you be, my love, without my
    discipline?'

Peck

A single kiss can lessen your life
Expectancy by three minutes. Doctors believe
Increased pulse rates during kissing
Strain the heart. Yet kisses have

Advantages, they're good for the teeth because
The saliva produced reduces plaque.
Kissing's a slimming aid too, every kiss
Consumes three calories.

The commonest kind of social kiss
Is the well-known peck on the cheek
In theatre college Stock Exchange club pub street.

Be warned, however, about this
Seemingly innocuous peck.
Some see it as the kiss of deceit.

And you may be pecked
By any bollocks you happen to meet.

Here Is Monica Now

Monica Ivors came up from the country
To make a living in town.
Disappointment made her realise
Anything is on.

So here is Monica now, nude
On a spotlit revolving stage,
Spreading her thighs for well-dressed men
Middle-aged.

She lashes herself with a whip,
Is lashed by a man with glasses
Who works all day in a bank.
Monica sucks him off.

Then in the darkened room
She lets two lit candles blaze from her cunt.
Extracting the candles, Monica
Lifts them high, the melted
Tallow jewelling her skin, shuddering
At each hot drop.
Taking three white balls
She stuffs them up her cunt.
Revolving-writhing for well-dressed men
Monica does not stint.

The first ball pops, Snow White,
The second, the Milky Way,
The third is streaked with blood.

Monica wipes that ball in a hurry,
Bows to the men and leaves the stage.
The money is good.
Good.

Lip-Service

That evening, having paid lip-service to my God,
I met a woman sniffing her husband's infidelity.
'Do you suffer' I asked 'from grief and rage in the blood?'
'I can cope' she replied 'so long as he doesn't tell me.'

It Must Be the Knitting *

'Most men's fingers are bad
At catching worms, worms laugh at men
But will come to a girl's fingers
As if they'd been lost and now they are found.
It must be the knitting, three hundred
Worms make ten pounds. Persuade a girl you can
Coin money from worms she coaxes out of the ground.
Worms can be more profitable than men.'

121

Us

'While he was riding me he kept gasping
Jesus Jesus as if he were praying
In the middle of it all, his breath rasping
My skin and hair, all his voices pouring

Jesus Jesus till he came into me
With one wild final sigh of Jesus
Then he fell away and lay
Like a child at my side. Jesus. Us.

A pair of people in a breathing room
Woman full of man
Man empty of woman

He asleep
She awake
Jesus gone.'

Stains

James Joyce gave up fucking for Lent,
Taking upon himself instead
Sole responsibility for washing
Nora Barnacle's bloomers clean of those red

And brown stains that so fascinated
Him. Joyce was into stains. Sin was a stain.
Shit was a stain. Piss was a stain. He felt elated
Every year when Lent came round again,

Giving him the chance to get rid of
All the stains of fucking, making Nora
Sleep with her head at the other end of the bed.

Then slowly, gravely, the old craving to love
Returned and Joyce spent Saint Patrick's Day
Fucking till he was nearly fucking well dead.

Cross of the Wood

Blood is the mother of thought
And thought the shadow of blood
Where Sebastian Conner is screwing
Sheila Noone at the Cross of the Wood.
In praise of her cunt his prick
Is a tremulous hymn,
Jesus is watching and listening
Thrown out of home
Condemned to wander the roads of the parish
Where Sebastian Conner
Would screw the moon
If the night was right
And Father Ignatius Flood
Is locked in a lush
Prayer-book fat as a Christmas goose
Waiting the knife.

The Way at the Time

'Are you surprised at the infant in the bag
Floating down the river in moonlight or daylight?
It was a servant-girl, you see, born in the bog,
Sent out at thirteen to work for a farmer,

Every penny of her sad wages went home
And she slaved away from dawn to dark.
When the farmer said "Come here, girl" she came
And when he said "Go back to work now" she went back to work.

And when he said "Lie down in the hay" she lay in the hay
And she said nothing when he emptied himself into her
And put a child making in her almost-child's body.

I saw many's the tied bag floating that way
In the river. She gave the best years of her life
To the farmer, her family. That was the way at the time, d'you see?'

Weekend

'Up for the weekend from Cork
To cheer on his heroes in red
He dropped in with two six-packs last night
Commandeered me for my bed.
We fucked, that is he fucked me,
And then, tipsy and bored,
He rolled off me like a bag o' wet spuds
And snored O dear Lord how he snored.
Erect Sunday morning at ten
He fucked me again and soon after
Downed rashers and sossies and eggs
Then left in a fat shower of laughter.
I'm a churned damp field, he's a plough:
Where is the spiritfuck now?'

I Suggest Joan Flood

'The main thing is to find someone to blame.
If we do that we'll put people at their ease.
I suggest Joan Flood, make her the focus of shame,
That'll quieten the tongues wagging in the cities,
Towns and villages of the land.
                              She's well known
As the best little ride in her own parish
Ready to open her legs for any man,
Cute little thing, shrewd, young, whorish,
Hated by married women, they'd love to see her nabbed
And put away for twenty years or so
Where she cannot lure a hubby to bed.
A whore in prison is as good as dead.
So get to work, lads. This case must be cracked
Within a month. Joan Flood is waiting to be
Convicted. Remember, an innocent child of God was murdered.'

Of All People

Though I'd rather be a tomcat than a theologian
(A tomcat spots a victim, knows how to waylay him)
I often ask myself why in the name of heaven
God created me in order to betray him.

I have no special art. There are times I think
I'm a simple turf-accountant at heart.

With his talent for absolute foreknowledge
And his position at the summit of immortal bliss
Why give me, of all people, the privilege
Of sending him up the river with a kiss?

Why not pick a woman, call her Judasena,
Cute little redhead with an iambic bum,
Man-conquering tits and a priceless smile
Fresh as Eve in yon garden of Eden, a
Gifted kisser of gods in kingdom come?
But no, it had to be me. I guess he liked my style.

Spiritfuck

'So many churches' she said, 'Such power, such polish
Because one man lived his conscious life.
Words are walls – Aramaic Greek Latin English French Polish
Etcetera; and my own anger freezing me stiff
In barren rooms of European and American
Cities. The day I heard that prayer
Means trapping the mind of God –
I a cage, he a bird of the air –
I understood the origins of my anger.

I sat alone and knew I had to open
Myself as I had never opened before.
I must be more open than any wound
Or any door
Anywhere.

I know spring water and polluted water
I know legends of love and loss
And the meaning of eat my body drink my blood.
I know the heart of the woman who yearned
For one true ultimate spiritfuck
Because I too long to be fucked by God.'

The Names

'The names he gives me

  good thing
    fast bit
      born whore
        tight cunt
          snazzy bitch
            would-be nun
              dirty slut
                sizzling witch
                  great ride
                      heart o' the home
                      snowy bride
                      randy spark.

Throw a bag over our heads

We're all the same in the dark.'

Get This

Open the door, see what's going on.
Get this: her brother is seventeen
Her father forty-one.
Brother and father fuck her

When they will, it's called abuse, but
No one can prove it.
One or two neighbours will tell you
The girl will grow to love it.

She loves the music of U2
And when only her heart is listening
She sings
Of red yellow purple green white blue
Of trees and the sea of love in the streets
And rivers wandering.

Who will open the door of her singing and crying?
Neighbours say she's all right; they're lying.

'Down we goes'

The Minister for Unemployment in Hell
Is scared shitless some Christian Jew or Turk
Will come up with the notion that people
Would like to work
And begin to believe in dignity.
The prospect is too ghoulish to contemplate
So he keeps the youngsters drugged and boozy
Crammed with frustration and hate.

'So down we goes to the Quay in Dunleary.
Fiona is locked outa her mind when Mick
An' myself decides to rape her. Jesus bleedin' Christ!

Me head bangs when I wakes in the mornin'.
I think I remember Fiona got sick
When Mick belted her face with his fist.
Ah sure the three of us were curse o' God pissed.'

An Unlimited Company

I saw the knife shape itself in the vast cold
It took an arsenal of cries to make the handle
The blade was made of unchronicled pain
Not of humans but of beasts and creatures
Without a name.
As it formed itself it swung slowly round in the air
Like a moon aware of its reputation for lunacy.
I stood there
And watched the knife select an iceberg in the freezing sea.
It pointed itself towards the iceberg and began to enter it,
Piercing, piercing like certain memories of living and dead.
Now the knife and the iceberg are an unlimited company,
The knife in the iceberg, the iceberg in the knife
In the freezing sea, kisses and bombs and fucks and
Sniggers and judgments in my head.

Lipstick-Letters

Nasty deeds and midnight secrets yanked into the light
Are no concern of mine.
My interest in melodrama is slight
Though spiced with elements of the divine.

Recently, however, I raised my head
On hearing why a randy
Friend of mine was dead.
He took a pretty thing to bed

Because she got him going in a pub.
They screwed till he felt sleepy-sick.
This proved to be an error.

She was gone when he awoke. In lipstick-
letters, large and red, WELCOME TO THE AIDS CLUB
Was scrawled upon his bathroom mirror.

If This Was Fake

There are as many heavens and hells
As there are men
But I discovered heaven in a moment
When I slept with Mary Magdalene.
To be honest, I didn't think I had a chance
But when I put my case
                        she smiled, said yes:
When she made love the world was love
And all her body did was bless
My body as I died inside her
And she lived as I'd never seen a woman
Live before. She gasped, cried, moaned,
                        shuddered, stilled.

Something in her stillness made me ask
'Mary, did you fake that orgasm?'
I'll never know. She kissed my cheek and smiled.
I smiled too, my whole body longing to sing.
If this was fake, Christ, what is the real thing?

The More Human

I meet a woman with one breast.
My eyes question her body, I get no answer.
I acknowledge the mastery of cancer
And know she knows that she and I are dispossessed
Midgets wondering can it please
Heaven to witness this disease.

The best way to fight cancer is to eat it.
I don't tell the woman this.
The clichés tell her how to beat it.
Cancer lusts for metamorphosis
As does your dispossessed adventurer
Through languages and clubs and scarce positions
And stale tales waiting to be freshly spoken

Amid paid gestures of articulate liars,
Priests and poets, experts, critics and professors.

Do I deserve inherited derision?

Does a chopped-off breast bleed its way to heaven?

What do they do with these breasts?
Burn them? Bury them?
Leave them for sniffing beasts?
Have the women forgotten
How they were kissed and bitten?
Will their history ever be written?

I say goodbye to this pleasant one-breasted woman
I am a one-purposed man.
Of the two, she's the more human.
We both live as best we can.

Kisses

What a noble sign of love is the simple act
Of kissing, especially the version lip to lip,
Implying passion no lover can retract
Without envisioning himself a hypocrite.
And are there not, in this love-ravenous world,
A hundred thousand variations
Of that blessed essential sign
Among individuals and nations?
I have kissed but little: here and there, a mouth,
An eye, a cunt and, now and then, an arse
To ensure that I became the thing I am –
Not the victim of some spiritual drought,
A human lump dumped in a ditch, scarce
Glanced at by good folk who don't give a damn.
But I, damn me, I give a damn, I always did,
My heart experienced metamorphosis
Of passion rampant in the blood
So that I knew what should be is not what is.

Whispering to deaf ears is profitless
As touching words like, has it come to this?
It has. Authentic prophecy is a lucky guess
And we are still confounded by a kiss
In the dark or half-dark or drunken light
With the evening dying at its own pace
Like an old man too knackered-shagged to dream,
Who has forgotten the lifesigns in his face
That years ago seemed angelbright
Before his eyes drank deep an evil gleam.
      Alfonsus John O'Grady, friend of mine,
Will not frenchkiss
A member of the slopposite sex
For fear he might asphyxiate the lady.
He has, as well, a passionate objection
To the notion of sticking his tongue
Into a fellow creature's mouth.
He does not think it wrong
But quite ridiculous and unhygienic
Believing that behind sweet flawless lips
Germs bide their slime, expecting fun.
The thought's enough to make Alfonsus sick.
Therefore, no frenchkissing. 'Why should I swallow
Other people's germs?' he asks, 'I've plenty of my own.
Do you know how filthy people's mouths are?
Have you ever opened her jaws and peeked in?
You'll wish you were a far hygienic star,
Between her teeth fester black lumps of sin.
If that's the sort of thing you wish to kiss
I wish you centuries of stinking bliss.'
      For all I know, not much, this may explain
Why Alfonsus John
Experiences a small, recurring pain
At the prospect of not being turned on
By wet tongues flickering between white teeth
Brushed silverbright with tasty fluoride,
Bodies randymad with juicy youth
Clamouring for the muff-dive and the ride.
Instead, O'Grady broods on the first time
His mother's lips kissed silk into his cheek,
The gentle affirmation of true bliss,
The sign that leads away from sin and crime,
The love that understands why man is weak.

Home is where the fart is, and mommy's kiss.
Kisses suggest emotion, a vastly
Complicated topic which I shan't go into now
Except to say it can have ghastly
Repercussions for the feeler and the felt.
I think of stab rip hack rend whip stick belt.
Sticky kisses of first love may help the whelps to grow
In confidence but their ferocity
Suggests a cannibalistic fury
Causing the approving heart to wilt,
Appalled such tenderness should lead
To such sweaty paddling in another's flesh.
Yet it is necessary, necessary
The young kissmunch each other,
The male one day may be a happy dad
And the object of his munching, productive mother.
Then stretch, young love, stretch limb and sinew,
In order to find out what's in you
The spittle-orgy must continue.
How many kisses
Have you received in life to date?
How many have you given?
Do you love your wife
Or are your kisses to her spiced with hate?
(Remember the first night?)
Do you kiss her out of duty or relief
Or just the sense you'd better get it over?
Compare this dutiful peck with that volcanic kiss
When you saw yourself a lover.
The insured years are enemies of fire,
Duty chokes desire,
She's standing at the door, she turns away
Knowing you've all to do, nothing to say.
You no longer wonder how it came to this:
A corpse is no more dead than a dead kiss.
A novelist, Hans-Christian Wurster,
Knocked at my bedsit door, came in
With a grin you wouldn't find in fiction,
Sat on a chair made by Joseph of Nazareth,
Sipped a cup of decaffeinated coffee
Said he wanted to write a blockbuster
About my strife and crimes.

Could he have a true
Heart-to-heart no-holds-barred let-it-all-hang-out
Interview?
He had his questions ready. They covered
Sex, violence, treachery, money, political intrigue,
The precise nature of the messianic impulse,
The passion to commit an ultimate sin.
'Well, Judas?' queried the decaffeinated grin.
'Fuck off, Hans-Christian' I said.
But he persisted. 'Wild horses
Won't force me out of here, Iscariot;
I'll not be shifted by car or bus,
By train, plane, donkey's cart or chariot
Till you reveal what my novel needs to know.
If you tell, you'll find it'll please us
Both. Why in God's name were you so
Brash as to plant a kiss on the face of Jesus?
Why choose the sign of love to be
The ultimate sign of treachery?
At that stupendous moment for mankind
Were you playing a game?'
I smiled and said 'One man in all this world
Understands that kiss, but modesty
Forbids me mentioning his name.'

      I once saw a modest kiss.
Herman's daddy took him to the zoo,
Showed him all the happy, trapped animals.
I was there too.
Herman called for an ice cream,
Sat on the edge of a pit
Containing several insatiable apes.
      Herman fell into it,
Broke a hand, a leg, was badly concussed,
Lay on his face, the apes slowly came.
One, a most ugly joe with great sad eyes,
Stood guard over Herman, kissed his head.
This world is not remarkable for modesty.
Herman was saved. I'm trying
To imagine the pain
Of a small, wild creature
Among trapped, happy men.

When the podgy sub-editor turned
And planted a long, boggy kiss
On the gob of the tipsy Foreign Correspondent
Pale from his recent act of Cosmic Analysis
But responding with some guts to Podge
I thought the Christmas office party
Would crapple in disarray
Since I believe in local manifestations of universal decay.
Instead, that minor orgy became a hearty
Free-for-all. I had nothing to say
As I watched the lads guzzling each other.
What would any decent mother
Think if she saw this sozzled riff-raff,
Normally a most efficient staff,
Discovering an old delight in a new way?
The birth of Christ sets Dionysos making hay.
I reflected, as I began to laugh,
I might have been ten million miles away
Nightmaring on a charcoal planet
Watching the sober Russians dressed in white
Breaking all records in the sunless light
Of image and politics and starwars hate,
Goading themselves to absorb the thought
It's possible to run where sun cannot obtrude
But works in other worlds far away
To warm the last drop of human blood.
The Russians have run faster
Than any man has ever run.
Each runner's penis swells in pain.
Unstoppable women charcoal from the dust,
Each woman takes a penis in her mouth,
Sucks, kisses, kisses, sucks, again, again.
How assiduous the women are,
How glad-insatiate. No almosts, no near-misses,
I marvel at their skilled procedure
As they confirm themselves sweet thieves of kisses,
Suckers of the Russians' come and go.
In that virgin charcoal land
I see again, as I saw long ago
On earth, women in command
Kneeling in blithe postures of submission
To the gods of love,
Tired, ecstatic runners towering above,

Becoming now a helpless shiver;
I saw this first in the time that is to come
When we're more equal than we dare to dream,
When betrayal accelerates martyrdom:
      Forgive me if I call it love,
      Something I misunderstand forever.
Beyond words, certain kisses promise much.
There was a lover
Who could never cease, never find peace
Till she had kissed his body all over
And over, breathing Holy! Holy! all the while:
Feet knees thighs lips cock balls belly buttocks
Shoulders chest lips lips teeth cheeks eyes
Head. Holy! Holy! Old women kiss a crucifix
Thus, as if purifying their shook lined mouths
Of the weighty self-important stink of men.
I've seen these women in dark places
Thrown out like empty wine bottles.
Once, they were held, kiss-tasted. Now they kiss an
Image of the dead god buried in their faces.
Empty bottles clatter, break, love's sacrifices.
      Yet I must speak of tenderness,
Soulbreath emanating in a kiss.
Am I imagining it, has this feeling
Vanished from the world? I think once
I felt it, long ago, an evening
Smell of apples in the air,
A sense of youngsters, believing in love,
Strolling among exciting promises there.
Perhaps it didn't happen, just one of
My illusions designed to sustain
A heart incapable of warmth.
For one moment, though, I might have fathered
A child coming home to pain,
Making his way, like dad, through storms
The battered dead have met and weathered.
      In the wars that are to come
Children of love, indifference and rape
Will perish with the earth on fire.
Not even a mythical idiot will escape
To kiss and kill a king because
The pain of learning is the learning of pain.
Is there anyone, anything, we cannot kill?

It is a source of satisfaction
To know not even the shrewdest creature
Can outstrip the terminal aspect of our skill.
We've spent our hearts for this, we spend them still.
Victims may kiss our feet, adore our blood,
Breathe homage into every lineament and feature,
Knowledge belongs to one, it always will,
Who dares to recognise, to kiss and kill his god.
                              I go out,
A calm evening, the kind that brings
The sick to beg release from pain,
Believers in miracles with a sense of what
Ought to be, persisting in hope.
My steps are slow, deliberate, I cover ground,
I cast a shadow, a not unfriendly shape,
My thoughts are skimming over all I've found
                              I come to him
I kiss the tired legends in his eyes
I kiss the pleading lepers in his face
I kiss the mercy flowing through his skin
I kiss his calm forgiveness of sin
I kiss the women hovering at his side
I kiss the men who make him their cause
I kiss the money made and lost in his name
I kiss the murders committed by his children
I kiss the mob adoring him
I kiss the mob killing him
I kiss the treachery of men
I kiss the ways they will remember him
I kiss the ways they will forget him
I kiss his words his silences
I kiss his heart
I kiss his caring daring love
                      He seems relieved
He murmurs something about a kiss
Betrayal
The Son of Man

I have never seen him so peaceful and still
Hardly breathing
As living creatures do

Has he ever lived at all?

Living not living
He is led away

I stand
Doomed with triumph
Nothing to say

> In the name of Judas
>> And of Judas
>>> And of Judas

> As it was in the beginning
> Is now
> And forever shall be
> Judas without end

> Amen.

Heigh-Ho

Judas Iscariot is buried and dead
Heigh-Ho buried and dead
And the heartbreaking worms work to nibble his head
Heigh-Ho nibble his head

Judas Iscariot has run out of cash
Heigh-Ho run out of cash
O give him a choice of the nail or the lash
Heigh-Ho the nail or the lash

Judas Iscariot has run out of hope
Heigh-Ho run out of hope
And he's casting his eye on this rogue of a rope
Heigh-Ho this rogue of a rope

Judas Iscariot would make a great cry
Heigh-Ho make a great cry
But he knows in his heart he'd get no reply
Heigh-Ho get no reply

Judas Iscariot with silence is one
Heigh-Ho silence is one
Questions and answers can't tell what is done
Heigh-Ho tell what is done

Judas Iscariot swings from a tree
Heigh-Ho swings from a tree
O he was the bad one the good ones agree
Heigh-Ho the good ones agree

Judas Iscariot grins at his doom
Heigh-Ho grins at his doom
Where did he come from? Out of what womb?
Heigh-Ho out of what womb?

Judas Iscariot is hanging alone
Heigh-Ho hanging alone
And no one can say where Judas is gone
Heigh-Ho Judas is gone

But I met an old goat who said Judas is well
Heigh-Ho Judas is well
And as long as that's true there's hope left in hell
Heigh-Ho there's hope left in hell

IX. I know I've arrived, can you tell me why I'm here?

A Dream of Keys

Down in the water among the black flowers
Among the Doolin dead the drowned boys' eyes
Like shining new pennies to entertain eternity

      The keys
Dangled ten centuries above my head
Like promises memories letters received and unwritten

      I said
These keys are mine   I will unlock

Myself healthy and sick

My father and mother my curses and prayers
My sex my sleep my relentless dreams
      My cute little arse

So I reached for the keys through the winter air
But they melted at my touch and threatened
      To burn my fingers, or worse.

As You Might Expect

My mother came to the tree
As I was hanging there
She began to cry
And tear her hair

      Greasy serpents of doom
      Slithered through her womb

I tried to open my mouth
No words came
The wind refused to help me
Say her name

                   I was born with a caul
                   My mother sold it to a fool

She broke out in grief
Accused the sky
Who killed my son? Who killed my son?

This, I take it, was love.

I continued to die
Hanging all alone, hanging all alone

As you might expect from the way
I'd been thinking, earlier that day.

I Shall Not Forget

I looked down on myself
After I hanged myself.
I took off my clothes,
The clothes of the hanged me
And carried them to a stream
Some fifty yards from the tree.
There, I washed
All the dirt out of my clothes,
I washed all the blood out of them
And all the sweat. I shall never forget
The smell of my own sweat.

Even if my mind is twisted for eternity
I shall not forget that smell,
My own smell, stronger than the thought of hell.

Even Now

Even now, out of the sexual dark,
        I could rise
And cut through the blindness
        Of my eyes,

Cut through the pathetic inevitable meshing
        Of men and women
In their God-ordained round-the-clock fucking.
        I could go on

And on through the sperm-riddled days
        And nights of those
Who love to increase their sorrows.

I could grope through fog to find what I never had,
        A glimpse cleaner than painlight
                Of the face of God.

Instead, my love my loss, I'll crawl home to bed.

Blueprint *

I must have been a thought in my own head,
Squatting there, innocent as cancer-seed,
Not giving a damn who was alive or dead,
Rehearsing my nature, designing the blueprint of my breed,
Growing up with the simple task of bringing
Heaven to its knees, the world to darkness
Until the light returned as, true
To its nature and function, it knows how to do.

I'm everywhere now, nobody's taking
Notice anymore. I'm not rare, I find it easy to reproduce
Myself. If I were my enemy, I'd have burned
That blueprint, but I'm not, my enemy is mankind
As imagined by a remote, noble spirit.
In the beginning was the freedom that let me happen.

I'll tell you this for nothing, my thoughtful friend:
The nature of God's freedom will never be grasped by men.
It's beyond all certainty and doubt.
I had to hang myself to find it out.

Dreams of Perfection

I know in my heart I never perfected
Anything. Yet, like your hand under my head
Supporting my brief sleep too long denied,
Conceivable, inconceivable universes focused in this bed,

Dreams of perfection visit me
Like thoughts of happiness.
I want to say, Come in, come in, you're welcome,
Stay as long as you like, your presence is a bless-

ing, I have lived to see you enter in-
to me; but no sooner are these dreams
here than they're gone like youngsters emigrating

      from places they'll always carry in their bones.
      O I've seen perfection all right, roses in slums,
      jewels rubbing noses with old County Council stones,
      but it slipped away from my grasp the moment I started
            half-thinking.
      I'm all flaws dreaming of some flawless thing.

End

Was all I did and said
To the end one man should die?
Dare I ever
Know why?
Of those who followed him
Who didn't lie?

Sounds

Again and again, that hanging night,
I heard the sounds of my life
Galvanising the grass.
                 My mother's cry
Came razoring my head.
The first time a teacher beat me
With a stick that sang through the air
Like a lark packed with venom
Choked celebrating bells in my blood.
                 The first bird I killed
Toppled into silence that was its own cry.
The sun melted and I begged
For the mercy in its light.
                 Words I didn't know the meaning of
Towered black and important as priests
In tall rooms of majestic loneliness
And unquestionable authority.
                 The words of a healing woman
Were so true I knew the sound of a lie.
                 When love threatened to drown me
With words so soft I knew they must be the opposite
Of God knows what
I sought the saving rumbles of beasts;
They taught me to listen to men
Whose hearts were rotten
Yet fine
Compared with mine.
These were pleasing sounds, silverbright.
I forget them now.
Only the sounds of a kiss in the evening light
Will not be forgotten.

Being Someone

I said to myself, Supposing my life
Were a comfortable overcoat
Capable of resisting the worst winter cold,
Would I have the heart to give it
To an old man shivering at
The edge of a village or in the dead
Centre of a Christmassy city street,
Shoppers lusting for goodies like Romans for blood?
      Suppose I were the old man himself
And a stranger charitied up to me,
Offered me his overcoat to keep me warm,
Would I accept this gift of seasonal love
Or would I look the stranger straight in the eye
With 'Fuck off, chum! Keep yourself free from harm'?
      Grant me the licence to be
A clown in a travelling circus
Fulfilling its destiny
Among the scamps and urchins of credulous
Provinces. There I bulge, waiting my turn,
My forehead so red the Big Top may burn.
Long ago I gave up daring to think.
Now, awaiting the ringmaster's wink,
I tumble through every laughable bone
Of my being into the swallowing eyes,
I'm Jackass, greased lightning, rainbow joke,
Bonfire Baggypants chuckling up in smoke,
Let me never again be conscious-awake
Cowed by what is and is not a mockable mistake,
But I am, and I look, and I lie
To the children escaping the massacre
For the moment, lost in the funny thunder.
      There's nothing as funny as a man
Who's not quite human.
That's why I cuddle the notion
Of changing from clown to Fat Woman.
      As a girl I was passably slim
But today these incredulous eyes
Feed on my boobs, my belly and quim,
My hot mythological thighs.

Tonight, for some reason, I'm feeling volcanic,
Vesuvius, Etna, my buttocks are fire,
My mind a pit of lava-thick rage.
Pardon me, please, if I heave and get sick
In this ring of my waddling desire.
How some women nosedive into old age!

In this me of deaf girls, autistic children,
Blind telephonists planning an evening of beer,
Rainy angels grey on the pavement
I am my own blind man whitesticking through hell
Wondering what my morning shave meant.

An elbow-touching apostle approaches:
'May I help you, sir, to cross the road?'
Impulsive charities arrive like despatches
From part-time soldiers in the army of God.

That morning shave has worked, I feel the wind
Fingering my face like a cosmic masseur.
Brother wind, are we not blind together
Or am I the blindest thing in this land of the blind?
'Thank you kindly for your help, dear sir,
I find it hard to manage this treacherous weather.'

A girl cursed me once, I whitesticked into her.
Soft flesh, yielding, granitecurse her voice.
Days come I choose to be made of stone
Drawn from a quarry where children play
Games that will be politics one day
When money is the marrow of their bones.
I am majestic outside a famous Bank
A top Insurance Company thrives close at hand
I am the most pigeoned monument in the land
I have survived the appalling human stink
Even of my creator who was paid to think
I am happy to survey the haste
Of the same old conscientious mob at work.
Perched on my right hand, a blackbird sings,
It is a thousand years from now, the blackbird wastes
Itself, a boy prepares to blow me up
Because old monuments are threatening things.

                    Being someone
Is strange. That untraumatic morning
Long ago, I knew I was no one.
I might have grown depressed, gone into mourning,
Taken to muttering in the tolerant streets,
Paraded my sensitive soul as an artist
Or poet up to his rhythm in debt,
Invaded Impressive Gatherings to get pissed
In the slumpany of Distinguished People,
Swallowed politics as Hitler's visionary sidekick,
Learned to deliver the most lethal
Insults to those who really hackle my wick,
Allocated Nobel Prizes to all who seem
To believe in some magnanimous dream
But I end up being this drably dressed
Non-being who can speak, gesture, smile
At others others others doing their best
To smile their way through the barely tolerable
Days, to hell with despair, so
I will not nag, complain or carp
At this idiot impulse to rise and go
Anywhere. I'm learning to play the Jew's Harp,
Neat touch, seems appropriate, besides
I've been informed that one of music's
Properties is deep, deliberate healing.
I may enchant non-beings on every side,
Provide a healthy interlude for the sick
If I play my little Harp with feeling.

O hear my music rise above the heads of men,
I play for... play for... Who am I, then?
A blind child stirs in me, begins to cry,
Her tears are mine, they burn, I don't know why
Her hurt is my heart, I must find her name
And let my music tell her who I am.
I must be someone, someone you'd say
Hello to, if I happened to pass your way.
My blind child cries, I believe she's near,
A moment, for a moment, let me know her.

Ringing the Baptist

I was working as an undertaker's assistant when I died
And was given the job of preparing my body for its coffin.
I sympathised with myself at my own wake, I cried
For myself, I reminisced about my life's performance:
Flawed, I concluded, could have been better.
I was, as you know, bald; a bald corpse.
I looked grey, hairless and dead, I thought it might be fitter
If I wore a new wig, so I rang John the Baptist,
He sent me one, made of the hair of his head.
I encountered some difficulty in affixing it.
I rang the Baptist again. He said 'Use glue.'
I did. The wig refused to stick. I felt mad.
I found a nail and drove it straight through my pate.
Wig fixed fast. I looked good, beautiful, true.
But for the nail I'd have been in a nice how-do-you-do?

Shy

Even my trusting darlings say I'm a cynic
Powered by self-loathing. Not so, my love, not so,
It is the age that's sick,
What sort of age will practise slavery
And call it freedom? What sort of age
Will sell itself for a bad dream
Then whirlwind into a rage
When one defines the nature of the crime?
I have a modest talent for definition.
Our natural element is the element we create
That is, pollution, though even in that climate
Someone doubtless finds himself saying 'I love you'
And he means it by God he means it.
Looking down on the city last night
In the shadow of an enduring tree
I saw what looked like rain but it
Wasn't rain, let me not say what it was, I'm very
Shy to admit some stinking truth I'm forced to see.

A disciple of the apostles has AIDS,
He was in Mountjoy Jail for six years
And now he's out, trying to get laid
By any scouting knockabout
He meets in the streets of the Capital.
'Mickser' I said, examining his eyes,
Aware that the most private part of a man is public
Though he be nicknamed after an archangel
Who has never fallen from grace,
'This will not do, this will not do,
You're sliding down the Capital drain.'
'Judas' said Mickser 'Give me some silver
And I'll refrain, yes, I'll refrain.'

If it be that I am guilty of self-loathing
Of the kind
That threatens the modestly defining mind
At such moments as we all recognise
It has to do with silver and what looks like rain.
If I hanged Mickser would that be a kind of loving?
Mickser is a prison full of cries
And hanging is an end to pain.
To-day in the Capital, no words but these:
'Help the handicapped, please! Help the handicapped, please!'

An Adjusting Experience

The morning after the Last Supper at which
Bacchic fracas some extraordinary things happened
I had a vision: a leper told me
One moment only of my life had mattered,
I was nearing the end of my allotted span,
My treachery, as it would come to be known
By those whose minds cut to the bone,
Played its own part in the divine plan
Involving birth, death, resurrection
And the redemption of man.

This vision was followed by voices:
First, a murderous peasant's: 'Cut out his heart';

Then a woman's, posh: 'Good idea, please hand me that knife';
And finally a chorus: 'He must be punished for his art,
Let's hack the creature into pieces,
Jolly slices of life.'

That is exactly what happened
Except that I, all alone in Croke Park,
Enjoyed a seat in the clergy-politicians' box in the Hogan Stand
Where I watched myself die, die,
Tiddly-i-die-die-die
                    at the hands
Of that beautiful butchering woman
Who knifed me with care,
Cutting off my parts and throwing them to dogs
Milling about, sniffing her, sniffing her.

It was hard to see a divine plan there.

To watch oneself being eaten is an adjusting experience,
It jolts the sense of perspective
So that one feels brutally sane
Despite being distributed among fangs,
Seeing titbits of self chewed and swallowed
With a gusto reminiscent of the judgments of men.

That's my last Last Supper by Jesus. Never again.

Creatively Buried

Like a slow poem my funeral moved to the Potter's Field
(I'd never looked that Potter in the face
Though people said the man was quite a case)
Where a few oddbods waited to sink me.

It was a pleasant day (I hate rain at funerals)
And just before the diggers committed me

To the Mother, several men in para-apostolic uniform
Balaclavaed out of nowhere.
Then, in a manner disciplined and stern,
They fired several volleys over my coffin.

If I weren't a corpse I'd have died laughin'.

These volleys made many people angry
Including bossy official apostles who called

For a full investigation
Into this gunning over the abominable dead.

But a Senior Apostle replied 'One must be practical.
Official intervention at para-apostolic funerals
Can cause a great deal of trouble,' he said.

The wrangling continues. I lie, creatively buried.

Spectator of Myself

As my dangling carcass swayed in the breeze
Beyond indignation and rage
I wouldn't toss you tuppence for your thoughts
On the implications of my body language.
But since I am a spectator of myself
Even at such post-ultimate moments
I could see poems novels saucy dramas
Flow from my undulating bones.

And, bless the mark, I could see soap operas
Of a murderously bubbly kind
Spread from the Potter's Field

                    to all the lands of the globe

Taking possession of millions of eyes
With garish lies capsizing the minds
Of young and old

                    till my story
                    is a weary
                    joke.

150

The Stony End

Nothing cracked my heart
until that evening
at the stony end
of the healing garden
when you turned and said,
as if remembering a secret
known long ago and long forgotten,
'I love you.'

Disinfectant

Such, at times, is my sense of my whopping
Soulstink, my spiritfilth, the cant
And raggy lies of my attempts at uttering
Myself, I buy a bottle of disinfectant

From a musical suburban supermarket
With a parking-lot as universal as the Catholic
Church, also, in its way, One, True and Holy.
I manic flatwards on my nagging bicycle

And drink the disinfectant
Like a priest gulping the blood of God.
A few minutes later, I'm a different man.

I vomit and defecate with prehistoric gusto.
I shudder and moan as a hell-purged soul would.
In three days I resurrect, an ordinary treacherous sonofagun.

Peeling the World

I washed my body with grace and water
It remained caked with sin
I spent seven days and seven nights
Peeling the world off my skin.

The world had penetrated my flesh
Taken possession of my blood
I let the dogs of my mind loose in there
They whimpered back, afraid.

In deepening terror I sought any part of me
That hadn't been world-stupefied.
No part could I find.

I was banklink cashsave monetary policy
Success failure eitherway too proud
To sweep the rubbish out of my mind.

By grace, by water I would be defined
But grace and water cannot make me kind.

Bad Company

I know a little about pain.
Bodypain, the tearaway thing,
Causes me to concentrate on the small
Of my back, hidden gut, such brain

As I possess. Not nice, must be endured.
I witness the mummified women
Sweating it out in the smelly corridors
Where nobody comes, neither the children they reared

Nor the men they tried to love. I find
A worse thing rending me, let me not bore you
With details, let me assure you
The demons screaming and shitting in my mind

Are everywhere like money
And bad company when they
Brag of making me their instrument of treachery.
If the demons make me, let the demons beware of me.

Never Be Short

Even the shrewdest biblical scholars are not aware,
As I kicked and jigged in my hanging position,
I decided to make a quick, mid-air
Act of Contrition.
Mother of Jesus, it worked like a charm.
My soul felt scrubbed and clean
And though assorted blood-vessels were exploding in my head
I was free of sin

For the first time since I was a nipper
On my mommy's lap of a Saturday night
Snug and purged after my weekly wash
And the old girl advised me to land a job with a pension,
Ignore groupies spouting mystical shite
And never be short of cash.

Whenever That Happened

Hell is the familiar all stripped of wonder.
Was there a moment
When wonder at the world died in my eyes?
Had I a friend I could recognise?
When did I take friendship for granted?
When did I get used to the thought of murder?
When did my flesh cease to astonish me?
When did my mind become grey-familiar?

Whenever that happened is when I knew
I could do anything.
When wonder died in me power was born.
I can change the world because I no longer dream of blue,
I can betray a god because I never heard a girl sing
Of steps in the street or sunlight blessing a field of corn.

Judasanity *

      Was it inspiration, rage or insanity
Caused me, that heart-freezing morning,
To found my own religion, Judasanity?
I clapped my hands, stamped my feet to fight the feeling
Of ice in the mind, flesh, blood, sinews, bones,
      And established my singular vision of things.
Would I attract the attention of even
A single soul concussed with the rights and wrongs
      Of living?

          Imagine my surprise when there came
Flocking to my spiritual banner
Hordes of people who believed they believed something else.

My countless followers rarely mention my name
But are faithful to my style and manner,
Pursuing, in their individual ways, the elusive silver,
Keeping Judasanity alive, protecting its pulse,
Distinguishing with infallible clarity between true and false,
Dancing to my tune, jigging my jig, waltzing my waltz.

You'll hear no music quite as true
As the music of you in me, me in you,
Two in one, one in two.

If You Will, Sir

Unlike many men who have mullocked through hell
And managed to gutter out again
I am not what bright people call cynical,
I am, instead, distressingly sane

And would learn German for the fun of it,
Gulp evening lectures on how to think
In a way that sheds a kind metaphysical light
On a mind accustomed to soulstink,

Bodystink, bloodstink, talkstink of demons
Whose sole purpose in death is to lead me astray
On a proven diet of cool, mocking laughter.

No, for me, hell is an education
Convinced it has something stylish to say
To poor souls. Interpret, if you will, sir.

Why Did I Cut Myself Down?

I spent last night in the company of the corpse
Of myself. I was strolling along my favourite
Pathway when I glimpsed my corpse in the twilight
Swinging from a tree. Oak, I venture to suggest.
Hopping over the hedge I cut myself down.
I was a sorry sight, my heaven-kissing eyes
Bulging with bloody dreams and prophecies
Or just popping in a way that suited the occasion.

I knelt by my self, looked me closely all over.
The grass was damp, I put my coat under my head,
I saw an ambitious youngster, a cold man. I could have wept
But didn't. I sighed. I saw a tentative lover
Of...who was she? He? I bent and kissed my dead
Lips. Then I lay at my side and slept.
When I awoke my corpse looked better, younger.

'That was a long sleep' I said, 'Maybe you'll tell
Me now if there's anyone alive or dead you ever
Loved as much as you wanted heaven and feared hell.'

That old sly look came back into my corpse's eyes.
I continued, 'Tell me, now that you're gone
Beyond this world of treachery and lies,
Are you part of the earth the sun the moon
Or some reticent star I've never dreamed of?
Or are you what the evidence suggests, mere dust?
If you'd rather not answer, I understand.'

'Do you?' grinned my corpse. Then, 'Whom did I love?
Retrospection is treacherous, there's the problem of lust,
I'm your past, your future, your only friend,
The last, vigilant spectator
Of what you have yet to suffer.'

I should have been consoled; still my anxiety grows.
Why did I cut myself down? Curiosity, I suppose.

Glint

Equipped with my Penguin *Iliad,* some German beer
And a goodly supply of potatoes
I went digging for myself. Down through four
Cities I dug though plagued by mosquitoes

And recurrent bouts of malaria. Beneath
The cities was an arena. I listened
And heard the heroes confronting death
In each other. Down through the arena I pen-

etrated for two festering summers till I found
A silver mask. I lifted it, saw my face,
Teeth perfect, jaw firm, eyes speculatively bold.

I kissed my lips in that most holy ground.
I was perfectly preserved, the mask was flawless,
My silver has a glint not known in Homer's gold.

It Is Done

Betrayed?

I betrayed
Nothing or what has become
Nothing worth
Betraying.

Or I betrayed
What lay beyond my comprehension
Puzzled me
Made me feel foolish
Made my understanding of things and people ridiculous.

I betrayed another kind of mind
A tolerant emptiness
An obsession with death
A style
A hatred of money
An addiction to folly
A rage against what is necessary and inevitable.

I betrayed an impossible attitude to the world,
An absurd approach to the ways of men,
A refusal to understand
The complexities of genetic engineering
Or the Master Race that must happen
When the loony-bins in the head are evacuated and burnt to the
          ground.

I betrayed a monster whose words would have crucified
The efforts and hopes of decent men;
Who would have me walk naked in a murderous climate,
Whose alternative to plague and the grey face of cancer
Lay in a fabricated lambasting of the self
And too much mocking spittle for comfort.

Comfort!
I betrayed a restless isolationist
Too guilty or hung-up to be comfortable,
Who never understood the primitive,

Cosy weekends of desire and fulfilment,
Who had a talent for fucking things up at the wrong moment,
Who could never accept the happy humming of the fridge in the
     kitchen
Or the plans, the plans for the bright brats of the future.

I betrayed
Spirit-killing organisation
And all its crawthumping fathers and mothers and daughters and
     sons.

I betrayed
The maker of the money-climate,
The father of the white bankers of international skill and concern
The sustainers of famine
The grotesque moralities of happy men
The Concorde sky of sophisticated mayhem
The angels of heavenly hospitality
And the whores and pimps of too-much-to-eat.

I betrayed
The origin of my own defeat,
The inspiration that caused me
To be.

And I did not betray
Myself.

What I did
Is done.

I am not one in three
Or three in one
But myself alone.

So cut to the bone, launch the ship, join the club,
apply the knife, tighten the knot, get the divorce,
measure the drop, kill the poet, honour the censor,
clinch the deal, organise the camp, advance on the birds,
find 'em fool 'em fuck 'em and forget 'em,
refuse to think, live in the land of the should-have done,
help me to see myself,
o for a bursary a house in the country

a well heeled centrally-heated sabbatical,
fix the count, arrange the promotions,
turn might-have-been into bitchery,
get into line, polish the cat,
stand back and let the dog see the rabbit,
o the style of that chancer and my Johnny on the dole,
watch the fiddlers at their music,
pay the bills, kiss the mortgage,
screw the system, praise the daubers, decorate the interiors,
say fame though you're lame is the name of the game
and never never fuck the begrudgers.

Be he damned or blessed
Whoever has done it will say
It is finished, It is done.

Ite, missa est.

I Meet Myself

After twenty centuries of vigilant sleeplessness
I am alive and well
As your average unfortunate traveller who has
Sidled through hell.
I thought I'd put an end to me
When I dangled like a doll
In my agony-ecstasy.
Ach! Not at all!

I meet myself in Houses of Parliament,
Brothels, churches, pubs, igloos, bungalows,
Funeral parlours where old friends lie in state.

I am solving a teenager's bewilderment
I am the first suggestion of an overdose
I am a whisper in bed to an opening mate.

The Howl

The mob's howl is blood
                 pouring between you and me,
A bomb behind a wall
                 where harvesters are meeting
To celebrate a fruitful Fall.

The mob's howl is hunger
                 making people dumb as minnows,
My first savage humiliation
                 in a room without windows,
Hardly the right training for a man.

It is a promise of no education
                 for children on the rack
Of ignorance taxed with despair,
Christmas decorations, imagination
                 shot in the back
Staggering off to die somewhere.

Yet sometimes above the howl there hovers a word
More heartening than any I've ever heard
As if the howl itself existed that there be
More than blood pouring between you and me.
Are we connected? How? If you can, let me see.
I'll connect with you. Who's guilty?

Mix-Up

An old woman of the roads once told me
The inadvertent switching of name
Bracelets in the Morning Star Hospital
Led to a baby mix-up in which some

Stupid nurse gave me away to strangers.
That moment of confusion deepens my life's irony
And causes my gorge to palpitate with anger.

I am not the man I am said to be,

I am someone else, someone else is me,
I wonder what he thinks of his position,
Does he know who he is in his swapped heart?

If I were in my rightful place would I
Have earned my dubious reputation?
Did earth and heaven con me from the start?

The allocation of name bracelets is a difficult art.

Becoming

I am becoming myself, a nothing, a myth,
Everything you'll ever want me to be.
There was that story of being born in Mexico,
Reared by serfs, bought by a touring lady,
Exported to England, polished at Oxford,
Stand-up comic in the BBC,
Got shingles, hit the drink, recovered,
Dabbled for years in a fashionable ology,
Converted to the Church of England for a while,
Was priested, opposed the ordination of women,
Fell in love, dear Mary, lost, managed to survive,
Took to fasting, perfected a hermit style,
Died in my chair one winter afternoon,
A fellow mythmaker swears I'm still alive
Somewhere in North Africa, waiting for the opportune
Moment to resurrect and call the tune.
Time, o ye demons, for a trueblue screw under the moon.

Let Me Be the Thing I Am

Above all, I pray you, do not fabricate me,
Don't make me a butt, a scapegoat, a paradigm,
Ne plus ultra, sine qua non, epitome
Of this or that.
                    Let me be the thing I am.
I'm not a dartboard to be darted at,
An old Nazi to be hounded, caught, tried,
Sentenced, hanged. I'm not Herod lying in state
Or Pilate turning aside.

I'm someone I don't know, yet I know this:
If you see my face blush till the blood
Is fit to break the skin while I try not to cry;

Should I shift from foot to foot, make choking noises,
Sweat like rain, disintegrate like faith in God,
Don't make my lie your truth, my truth your lie.

Future Guilt

The mountain is judging me tonight.
I've been hauled here into the Black Valley
And made to stand before that tribunal.
A few stars have scurried away in terror
And hidden their faces in darkness beyond darkness.
The moon spits, gives a sneering grin
That in a tick disfigures time and space.
What is my sin?

The mountain is listening.
Some new stars are giving evidence,
Their faces made of hate, their tongues filthy.

The jury of planets doesn't miss a thing
And the verdict makes sense.

Guilty. The mountain repeats it. Guilty.
I will be sentenced in the Black Valley.
When I hear it pronounced in appropriate tones
I don't know what to make of the sentence:

I'm to bear the weight of the mountain's shadow
Till my blood vanishes and my bones
Melt. Wherever I travel on earth
The mountain's shadow will be mine.
Day and night in sun and wind and ice and rain
Nothing I do will shake it off.
The more I struggle to be free
The more it will burden and entangle me.
I must never protest or question
Because when the mountain passes sentence
On a man, it's the end, or the beginning, as you will.
The shadow I cast now is mountain-huge, and growing still.
If follows me like future guilt,
Stretches before me like my past
A malignant judge who'll never rest
Till he's convicted me of waste
And sentenced me to a black hole
In the middle of my heart:
I'll be a lump of writhing dust
Hating the thought of what I am.

Therefore, one evening, late September,
Sauntering down an empty street
I strangle my own shadow.
          I do, I know I do.

Forever and forever I'll remember
My strangled shadow in the mild light.
If shadows die this death is true.
If not, shadows lie too.

Arrived

Judas, my age my love my self my art
My mortgage my job my pension my memoirs
My dreams my critic my radio my pen
My eyes my words my words

Refusing to say me, saying there's nothing to say,
Slipping down laneways like poets who know
Poems are no longer needed and little apples
Won't grow some later day.

Judas my school my holiday my official reading list
My summer job my fourth world my plan for killing pigeons
My books my footnotes my arthritis my inner city
My pub my career my bit on the side my plans for retirement
My lump of concrete flung from the terraces
My broken bottle in this drinker's grip
My nuclear reactor my shrink my greed my fear
My hands my lips my tongue my stink my mortality.
I know I've arrived, can you tell me why I'm here?

x. Some lads

Out there in there

Bomb is tired squatting there, doing nothing,
Just waiting for that ultimate ecstasy.
This morning, Bomb said it was planning
To play with modern poetry.

'Out there in there where the last word won't go
Where no word has ever been
I would like to hear a poem ticking
Like my heart. Let the Tick
Be tender blunt uncouth obscene

I will study it more mercilessly than anyone
Has studied me. Tick, tick, I will make
That tick my own,
Plant it in a word I will menace into being,
A word to do with known, unknown,
In me of me beyond me
Breeding a new ancient poem
Tick, tick,
I will study
Until it merges with my bone,
Bonepoem, bombpoem,
One-word-poem-tick-tick-way-of-seeing
Into the flash that is beyond all believing.'

Guess

I met Gee-Gaw Chatterton in Holland.
He's a traveller through the world. He told me
The best way to raise cash nowadays
Is through forgery. Gee-Gaw had forged three

Copies of the Kabala, two of the Koran
And was at work on *Much Ado About Nothing*.
This he described as throwing the shit in the fan.
I decided to try my hand at forging

One of the Four Evangelists, masters of bonny prose
Who translate badly but get a grip on people's minds
With their fetching versions of that remarkable story.

I set to work, I toiled for heady days,
I sold my finished text. Flawless. Scholars find
It magnetic. Which of the Four is it? Guess. Go on. Try.

Terms of Revelation

Professor O'Paytreat is getting eighty thousand
Sterling
For a preface and postscript to The Sparrow Edition
Of *Ulysses*.

Professor Tegrotty has signed a contract
For three million dollars flat
And a monthly expense account of twenty thousand
For a life of Sam Beckett.

And what in God's name is the life of Sam Beckett?
Don't we all know he taught French, played cricket,
Joined the Resistance, got stabbed, wrote books,
Was economical with the truth?

And what about me? It ain't fair, feck it,
Who'll pay me for my poem about
My investment in God and other ticklish matters?

Who'll reveal me to the lewd-studious mob
In a preface an intro a shamelessly honest biog?
When terms of Revelation are legally agreed
How much will the bugger get paid?

The Dinner

James Joyce had dinner with the Holy Family
One Saturday evening in Nazareth.
Mary was a good cook, her Virginsoup was delicious,
Joyce lapped it till he was nearly out of breath.
The Holy Family looked at Joyce who said
Nothing, he was a morose broody class
Of a man, his glasses made him look very sad,
It was next to impossible to get him to talk and
The dinner was uncomfortable as a result.
'How're things in Ireland?' asked Joseph. 'Ugh' said Joyce.
'What're you writing now?' persisted Joseph, 'I couldn't find fault
With your last book. Perfect.'
                                Joyce seemed to sulk.
'A large work' he muttered, 'Like the Bible. The sea. My voices.'
'Am I in it?' queried Jesus. 'Yep' said Joyce 'Pass the salt.'
'Is it too much to enquire about the rôle I play?'
Continued Jesus. 'It is' said Joyce.
Mary changed the subject. 'Are there many grottoes to me
In Ireland?' 'Countless' replied our hero.
Joyce's short answers were buggering the dinner up.
'The Society of Jesus' queried Jesus 'How's it going?'
'Who knows Clongowes?' said Joyce 'Could I have a cup
Of Bewley's coffee to round off this occasion?'
'Why did you leave Ireland, James?' queried Joseph,
'The Swiss, French, Italians are just as lousy
In their ways.' Joyce pondered. 'Crime'
He replied, 'Of non-being.' Jesus butted in:
'In that case you must have sinners in plenty.
I think I should visit Ireland, sometime.'
'I wouldn't, if I were you' said Joyce.
'But you're not me' said Jesus 'Though there
Are times when you behave as if you were
The Son of Man Himself. You get in my hair,
James, from time to time, with your pretentious
Posturing, sitting on a cloud, paring your toenails
In an orgy of indifference, pissed on white wine.
Though I readily admit your prose is divine
With touches of Matthew Mark Luke and John,
Why can't you be an honest-to-God
Dubliner, go for a swim in Sandymount, spend

Sunday afternoon in Croke Park or Dalyer,
Boast of things you've never done,
Places you've never been,
Have a pint in O'Neill's,
Misjudge the political scene,
Complain about the weather,
Miss mass, go to Knock,
Take a week in Killarney,
Listen to McCormack's records,
Re-learn to mock, jibe, scandalise, sneer, scoff
And talk your head off.
James, you have a block about Ireland,
You're too long on the continent.
In some strange way, James, you are,
If you ask me, bent.'

'But I didn't ask you, Jesus' replied Joyce,
'It so happens I think things out for myself,
I had to leave Ireland to do this
Because no one in Ireland has a mind of his own,
I know that place to the marrow of its bone
And I insist that people are dominated by your henchmen,
Those chaps in black who tell folk what to think.'

'I beg your pardon' said Jesus 'These men
Are not me.'
            'Would you put that in ink?'
Asked Joyce.
            'In blood' Jesus replied.

'This is getting too serious' Joseph interrupted.

'Shut up, Dad!' said Jesus 'The matter *is* serious.
It's precisely for this kind of crap I came and died.'

'But you're alive and well, son' Joseph said 'You're not dead
And we're the Holy Family. That's what they call us.'

'What family is wholly holy?' asked Jesus.
Joseph looked about him, then at the ground, perplexed.
That honest carpenter didn't seem comfortable.
There was nothing he couldn't do with timber
But this was a different matter.

                              He said nothing,
Just poured himself another cup of Bewley's coffee.
Mary said, 'Let's finish with a song,
Mr Joyce, I understand that you
Took second place
To Mr McCormack at a Feis.
But that's a long time ago, a long
Time ago.
Though second place is not the place for you
Perhaps you'd give the Holy Family a song.'

Joyce brooded a bit, took a deep breath,
Straightened his glasses gone slightly askew,
Coughed once, then sang *The Rose of Nazareth.*

The Holy Family loved his voice.
It was pure and clear and strong,
The perfect voice of the perfect sinner

And the perfect end to the dinner.

Every Decent Family ·

Every decent family should have a brothel attached
Instead of a half-hearted garage.
How else can they be expected to survive
In this age of hate and rage?
Keep a whore instead of a car
Your man is happy
Driving her to work
Nearly every morning of the year.

The whore keeps the wife alive
The wife hates the whore
The whore screws the man, the man loves the wife,
It is always possible to entertain a guest,
The garage boasts old tyres and plastic bags
Though there are times when the desire to burn
Everything to the ground can scarcely be suppressed.

A Game Lad

Pontius Pilate did his Ph.D. on the theme of
Crucifixion in the Post-Post-Modern Novel.
He ensconced himself in the British Museum
And waded through oceans of relevant material
Much of it, sad to relate, drivel.
But Pontius persisted for he was a game lad
Pouring, year after year, body and soul
Into the task; and he came up with the goods.

The External Examiner, Oxbridge man,
(No equal in the field,
It was agreed)
Gave the Governor a rough passage in the oral exam
Yet, in the end, he covered Pilate in glory
Noting, in his report, that here was a fine
Scholar incapable of even a teeny-weeny sham,
An academic colossus who'd doctored the authentic story.

No Time for Answers

Of the dubious creatures slouching on this earth
Flanagan intrigues me most:
He'd edit Nature, adjust the nameless planets,
Sell bibles to suburban housewives
Then give them the fuck of their lives,
Make a cock's hat out of the Holy Ghost,
Demonstrate the exact ways in which anarchy is order,
Explain why Judas is not a popular Christian name
Explain the fallacy of fame
Breakfast on the morality of murder
And discourse on the origin of the sense of shame.

Turning on me those eyes which on this winterday
Are marine green daggered by freezing blue
He asks 'Judas, what is fear?'

This is no time for answers, I snake out of his way,
Here's an airport ticket, I'm gone, where am I now?
Wherever it is, thanks be to Jesus Flanagan isn't here.

The Wrong Finger

On one of these divine mornings
That never fail to augur well
For blind mankind, I attended the wedding
Of Heaven and Hell.
Hitler and Eva turned up, I sat with Marilyn
Who was pregnant with delight.
Heaven sublimed in a skyblue suit.
Hell was all in white.

The world was a church that morning
The congregation, drawn from history and myth,
Emitted gasps of adulation.

Hell blushed when Heaven slipped the ring
On the wrong finger but we all drowned in joy
Knowing without contraries is no copulation.

A Rough Honeymoon

Heaven and Hell had a rough honeymoon.
Hell had a sense of humour
That Heaven frowned on:

> *There was a conductor called Hass*
> *Whose balls were two small spheres of glass*
> *Which tinkled toccatas*
> *And fugues and sonatas*
> *And on Sundays the B Minor Mass.*

Heaven didn't like Hell's banter
And exhorted her to be more serious.
Otherwise, said Heaven, the world will think you're a cod.
Fuck the world, said Hell, I believe in God.
Heaven pushed on: Your breakfast jokes are vulgar.
'How do you like your eggs?' 'Unfertilised.'
That sort of crack is in bad taste.

Perhaps it is, conceded Hell, but we must get to know each other
And jokes point the way to the heart of the matter.
Let's reconcile me laughing with you being scandalised.
Otherwise our marriage is a bit of a waste.

The Main Thing

Heaven and Hell were at a dinner-party one night
And met Micky Moggerley and Sheila Nagig.
'How's the crack in Leeson Street?' said Sheila to Heaven.
'Fine' replied Heaven, 'though Hell is a bit of a prig

And objects to whores shunting up and down
That sparkling thoroughfare'. 'Well then,
I wouldn't worry too much about that' said Sheila
'Whores have a funny effect on women and men.'

'Don't they, though?' mused Heaven. 'It's almost as if
Whores were men's mothers in dreams,
Laying the whole deal on the line once more.'

'Hadn't thought of it that way' said Sheila,
'I wonder if that's why Micky, at times,
Makes me pretend I'm his mummy first, then his favourite whore.'

'Keep it up, Sheila' said Heaven, 'the main thing is don't be a bore.'

Smiling Hell

Don't you like my savage smile? smiled Hell,
Isn't it more renewing than yeast-free Vitamin B?
Doesn't it make you feel hellishly well
After you've been split in pieces by

The ravages of good living? Have I
Not seen you glum and lonely on virtue's path
Stepping painfully on the callous gravel
Crushed by goodness and your heart's pure worth?

Ah you are a perceptive devil, conceded Heaven,
You notice many things untainted souls ignore
Though you stink of double-think and vile guile.

One must be what one is, grinned Hell, that's one
Sure five or six, I am what I am, more
Or less, I'm glad you've grown to like my smile.

Put the Kettle On?

'...till death do us part' mused Hell, 'Fascinating phrase!
Till life do us part might be more fit or
It might not. Death gets all the blame these days
For the bad sunderings. But you will never

Part from me, Heaven, will you? If I should
Set up drunken residence in the gutter
Where I feel most at home, whiskey in my blood,
Victim of the filthy truth, mistress of the bitter

Word, stinking ten times worse than usual,
Nailed with the worst name ever spittled in this town,
Whoring in quayside dives that make you frown
Because they separate God from man

And woman, will you, dear Heaven, when all
The known universe has cast me down
And out into universes unknown,
Please whisper, 'Darling Hell, rise up, come home, I'll put the
        kettle on?'

And Heaven replied: 'I may, and then again, I may not,
But I probably will, my little infinitely stinking pet.'

Best Interests

The marriage of Heaven and Hell was bound to crack.
Incompatible, that's what they were, querulous and wild.
When they split, therefore, it came as no shock
To those in the know. Heaven and Hell had one child,

A boy called Navv, that's the Irish for Heaven.
The pair went to court to contest custody.
The judge, who knew both parties well, said
It was in the boy's best interests to go to Hell.

Heaven looked haggard as he brushed past reporters
And later announced from one of his many mansions
The judge had taken him for a ride.

Hell, by contrast, smiled divinely on all comers.
Dressed in white, angelbright hair swept back in a ponytail,
She strode from the Court, laughing, little Navv at her side.

Best of All

Flanagan thought he was Jesus Christ
And Sylvester White was the devil.
Flanagan took a scythe and sliced
Sylvester down the middle.

'It's all over' said Flanagan, 'the world is at an end.'

He wiped the scythe with a fistful of hay.
'There now! The devil is dead, I am man's only friend,
The light, the life, the scythe, the truth and the way.'

Psychotic, the doctors agreed, that's what Flanagan is.
Guilty, concluded the jury, but insane.
Lock him up, growled Sylvester's ghost, throw away the key.

Why must people always want to be Christ
Or the devil? Why can't a man be a man?
Or, best of all, why can't a man be me?
Murderous romantics must be contained, you see.

A Bottle o' Brandy

'an' there was the poor fucker in the hospital bed
dyin', an' the doctor had told him five years
before that if he didn't give up the jar
he'd be dead
in no time. Well, he lasted exactly
five years gettin' pissed out of his mind
in cities all through Europe an' America
but of course he came back to dear old Dublin

to die 'cos it's a marvellous bloody city
to get corpsed in. This was accomplished
for your man when a lifelong friend

smuggled in a bottle o' brandy
to the hospital, your man drank it like a shot
an' that was the end, my friend, the glorious fuckin' end.'

poemprayer

he escaped then from the prison of his body
out into the decent air
leaving behind the pathetic rubbish
that was all right in its own way
and he made a poem to his Lady
that was a true and beautiful prayer

this poem was made out of all his longings
scattered like shells and stones on the shore
it was made of moments after lies were told
and he feared love might be no more
it was made of words lost at night and the tired eyes of women
and shadows gadding on the kitchen floor

it was made of moments of betrayal and wonder
and mockery and slander and pain
it was made of dead friends and enemies
and stories of this man and that woman
it was made of every defeat he had faced or ignored
and hurts known and unknown

today i heard an old man say the poemprayer
in a clear strong voice
that turned this battered world for a moment
into a warm-hearted house
and the clouds of heaven and the stones of the road
were glad to rejoice

The Right Colours

Flanagan asked me if I'd paint the room
The right colours for him.
He might settle in that room, he said, he'd been
Wandering a long time.
Red, I said to the men. They painted red.
It looked good. Yellow, I said.

They painted yellow. Green, I said.
They painted green. I stood

Back. It was a different room, it was wrong,
It stank of betrayal, someone was crying
Behind walls, the air began to bleed.
Black, I said, black it all, the whole damned thing.
They painted black. The room stopped lying,
Told its truth. Black is your man, I said. Flanagan agreed.

Relic

Myths flutter thinking wings about a man,
Theorems from Euclid, plans from Pythagoras.
Of the stories concerning Flanagan
My favourite, epic in its way, has
To do with his Aer Lingus pilgrimage
To the Holy Land where he went on the piss.
Out of his mind, Flanagan had the urge
To bring a relic home that would impress
A hosting of fellow-mythologists.
So off with our hero to the Potter's Field
Where he dug me up. I was less than beautiful.

Flanagan didn't mind. He bagged me. Back home, pissed
At parties in his flat, he drank poteen
Amid a giggle of myth-makers out of my skull

Swearing
As he sucked the good stuff
Through the holes of my eyes
That only a drink from the skull of Judas
Will make an Irishman wise.

Upset

Pilate, darling, I'm upset all day
I didn't want to wake you in bed last night
I had a dream of the man's innocence
I want to speak out
I saw a flower in the middle of a field
I saw weeds organised like armies
Black battalions closing in for the kill
              I saw a cheese-and-wine party
You'd gathered ambassadors and their wives
            At a jolly function to celebrate
Styles of conquest in different lands

I told you about the flower, the weeds in murderous waves
Converging.
            You turned peevish.
'Fetch a basin of water, woman' you snapped
'My hands are filthy, I want to wash my hands.'

An Exemplary Guest

Whenever Hitler visits my bedsit
I share with him my views
On the family customs, sexual habits
And business skills of the Jews.

I find him an exemplary guest,
Quiet little man, likes to shave closely,
Circumvent his moustache, choose
His few words precisely:

'Please, no trouble on my behalf, I'm just
Happy here, thank you.' He goes to pains
To compliment me on my conversation,
My self-portrait, my home cooking and baking.

I feel at ease here with this gentlest of men
Though sometimes outside my door I get the notion
Someone is quaking.

Winston Added Brandy

Whenever Hitler discourses on the skill
Necessary for war and the extermination of the Jews
He reflects at length on Winston Churchill
And that great man's epic love of the booze.

Winston, says Adolf, hated the taste of water.
It had an emaciating effect on his mind
And might have tampered with his plans to slaughter
The infernal enemies of humankind.

Therefore, adds Adolf, Winston added brandy,
Never in a craven way, to every glass
Containing water. This made him brainy, brave,
Inventive, witty and occasionally randy.
Churchill, moans Hitler, shoved bombs up my ass.
Drunk as a skunk, he learned how to behave
In ways that brought him his immortal glory.
Now, if I'd behaved like that – a different story!

Through a Pleasing Mist

One dreaming morning through a pleasing mist
In the Garden of Eden I saw Adam
Pissed.
At first I was tempted to kid him

But noticing a knifey look in his eye,
Refrained.
'Christ, Judas' he moaned 'I'm fit to die!
That cider! It's bombing my brain!'

'What cider?' I asked.
'All the little apples of Eden' Adam replied
'I made cider of them, drank the lot.'

He puked. 'That's knowledge' I remarked.
'That's cider' he wailed, 'Bad cider.' 'Knowledge' I insisted.
Adam sobbed. 'Knowledge or cider' he wept, 'It's all bloody rot.'

So Many Names

'Hello, Judas, you whore's melt!'
Is how this jumped-up knacker
Flacks my eye this trumped-up morning
In this snakey place, this bad corner
Where knackers nurture insults like grudges
And fling them at me...why?
Whore's melt? How solid was the lady
To begin with? With what spark did she lie
To spawn me, scapegoat, sinbag, spat-on-myth?
What was the deciding factor when he fucked her?
What did she look like in her sweating pelt?

This prick is right
But I hate him like the sin I'll commit
To give him and his breed the chance
To christen me whore's melt. I have
So many names, names by the bitter score.
Before you were born, I had foul names,
Each name vile as a leper's sore.
There'll be more.

Scared Shitless

I ran into Hitler escaping from Berlin
Scared shitless, that's understandable, not knowing
Which way the winds of revenge were blowing.
'I've decided' he said 'To come to Dublin,

Good Catholic city, people are just and fair, a
Real advantage to me in my present position.
I'd be honoured to meet Mr de Valera
If you could arrange it, Judas. He's one man

Who appears sympathetic to my cause,
A frequent caller at the Embassy
Enquiring if my Mission is going well or not.'

'I'll do my best, Hitler' I said 'But for Jesus'
Sake please lie low for a while. I'm trying
To nab all Nazis. We Jews are a sticky lot.'

Restraint

Though Flanagan's acting style is not in fashion
– Such volcanic words! Such knottings of the brow! –
He was asked to play Jesus in the Passion
Play at Oberammergau.

Flanagan accepted, rehearsed the part for months.
                    On opening day
As Flanagan-Jesus staggered under his cross
                    On the way to Calvary

An amateur assassin stepped out of the crowd,
          Spat on him, punched his face
          Screaming 'You perfidious fucking Jew!'

Jesus-Flanagan restrained himself. His voice, when he spoke, was
                    not loud.
          'Wait' he hissed 'Till after the Resurrection
And by Jesus you'll see what I do to you!'

Trial by Television

Pilate objected to the television show
Close-upping his washed hands as though
He had no real interest in being just.
'When people see that show' he said, 'They must

Conclude the Roman Governor doesn't know
How to govern. Look at it! The accused stands there
Looking noble, the mob lusting, the climate grow-
ing murderous, myself seeming only to care

For my own comfort, wanting to be rid
Of this chap, please the politicians and priests,
Wash my hands clean of the entire messy affair.

I'm shown in the worst possible light, a spineless sod,
A well-dressed nincompoop who simpers and bleats,
Jesting 'What is truth?' and won't even wait for an answer.

I'm tried already, sentenced to blame for Calvary,
Schoolkids will jeer me through all eternity
But show me the man who knows the whole story.'

'Too bad, Pilate' I said, 'You are what you're shown to be.'
'O Christ, Judas' anguished Pilate,
'Is the whole damned show TV?'

The Last Question *

As the programme petered out
And millions yawned towards bed
And that state of cosy repose
Popular with the dead

      He asked me the last question:
'What, now that you seem
To have achieved your goal, would you
Like most of all to do?'

This threw me. I squirmed in a way
That suggested I was thrown or had
Received some unexpected curse or blessing.

I gathered my resources and replied,
'I would like, until my time has come to go,
To keep the prophets guessing.'

The Calvary Crisis

Crucifixion is depressing but it makes
Fab television especially if it's a rainy
Day at the seaside or near the Black Lakes
Where you repose in hope of becoming less weary
And bored with tedious accounts of endless
Catastrophe.

             Sky News' minute-by-minute
Coverage of the Calvary Crisis
Together with the Beeb's incisive and comprehensive
Bulletins should keep you up-to-date
With every detail
Of this horrific but fascinating event.

There'll be an open discussion on the Late-Late
Show, dealing with some if not all
Of the consequences. Don't miss it. I won't.

Isn't it like getting a promise from the Son of Man
That we'll never be bored again?

Understandable

On a package tour through eternity
I met Christopher Columbus trying to discover
Something. Isabella, Queen of Spain, shrewd lover,
Gave Christopher the cash to find the Indies
In the Santa Maria, the Niña, the Pinta

But he stumbled on the Bahamas instead.
Christopher and his crew had almost died
Of these diseases you meet when you're at sea.

It is understandable, therefore, that his men
Should set about raping the Indian women
And by the grace of weapons shedding some Indian blood.

'Out here in eternity you've had time to brood on
Such matters' I said, 'What did you bring these people?'
Christopher smiled: 'Pox, poverty and the word of God.'

Holiday

Exhausted after the Fall of Man
I packed my bags of sin
And took a fortnight's holiday in hell
Hoping to find my origin –

al soulgusto. In the lower depths I ran
Into Charles Stewart Parnell.
He looked tired and sad. 'The Bishops spun
A yarn about you' I remarked, 'Your whole

Dream of a humane island was wrecked.
Isn't love wicked? Eunuchs' envy is fierce.
They nailed you to their Celtic cross despite your gritty

Fight. You poor thing! You still look shocked.'
No words. And then 'I am' he said, 'What's worse,
Though I scour every hole in hell, I can't find Kitty.'

Patron Saint

There should be a patron saint of rubbish dumps
Especially when rubbish dumps are people
Who receive a stunning overall majority
In the election of Baduns to take all
The blame for crimes accomplished and imagined.
In a world aglow with perks and privileges
You'll understand how nakedly deprived I feel
In the matter of certain small advantages.
        I've been a rubbish dump a long time now,
Hungry gulls alight on me to pick
Choice morsels of guilt, blame, recrimination, remorse.

I think of my patron saint's illumined brow
Listening to my prayer mumbled from centuries of shit
But all he hears, clean Jesus, is an old reeking curse.
If my patron saint won't hear me right, who will?
If prayers are curses in my mouth, why should I talk at all?
If blood is spilled, blood must be chosen to spill.
If men believe they're fallen, someone must exemplify the fall.
Suppose I change places with my patron saint
And he has reason to mouth a prayer to me
Shall I listen and reply? Shall I ignore him?
Choke the words in his throat? Pretend his words are true?
Suppose he has a problem as some saints do
Shall I give the man a compassionate hearing,
Assure him he's not a rubbish dump, a condemned house,
A homesick unemployed AIDS-blasted male prostitute
Subject to cruel tirades of public jeering
('You'll be buried in the arsehole of Tubberneering')?
Shall I open to his pleading, soon or late?
No, I'll be myself, must be, locked self, locked Judas.
O saint of God, what man dare know thy state?

The Light of Men

I saw the light of men in the corner
Of a pub. I was doing the crossword
In the less backward of our evening papers
When a tipsy out-of-work actor

Began to mumble about his lives.
Out of his eyes shone the life that is the light of men
Exhumed from dark theatrical archives
Where old gods snore in the Equity den.

Aspiring gods are gone on strike
Looking for better conditions in heaven.
Hell is satisfied with itself. Well, hell, why not?

The light of men is a laser beam through my mistake,
I read the signs, billions unborn wish to get even
With me. My mind is clear. I'll be here after all the actors rot,
Doing the crossword in the adjudicating light.

Special Decree

'I, Judas Iscariot, am assuming special powers
to take over the authorship of this Book
from my collaborator, Brendan Kennelly, who is a sick man.
I will be working with an Emergency Committee
to run the Book while he is unwell.
                                        The Lads and I
sincerely hope he will soon be better, and that
he'll be able to finish the Book without much
further help from us, once his health improves.
His work on the Book has taken its toll: he's suffering
from exhaustion and judasfatigue, and is presently
convalescing at his summer retreat in Ballybunion. We will
of course let you have further news of his progress.

Until he returns, we will need to make certain changes
to maintain the smooth running of the Book.
Captain Flanagan will be responsible for law and order
in the Poem, assisted by his deputy Major Dicky
(late of Portlaoise) and his team of voluntccrs.
All religious matters must be now cleared with
Cardinal Caiaphas, representing the Bishops of Ireland.
Literary allusions will be controlled by the Ministry
of the Interior, headed by Mr Harry Novak, who'll have
special responsibility for compound words, neologisms,
references to sheep, puns and other acts of linguistic treachery.
The Ministry of Plagiarism under Mr Barabbas
will look after thefts and borrowings from other books.
Mr Hitler here will deal with your questions, and has
already decreed that question-marks are now banned,
so there can be no questions. I am taking over
personal control of the first person singular.
I am sorry to have to tell you that Dr Pilate
has decided to step down, for personal reasons.
He wishes to spend more time with his family.
We will have to proceed with the Poem without
the benefit of his sound judgment of a line.'

Judas and his Apostles faced the Press
and several Renaissance artists in the Upper Room
from a long table lined with loaves, chalices,
bottles of Bulgarian Red, and clusters
of microphones (which the painters chose to ignore).
As he was wishing his fellow author a speedy
recovery, an armoured car and a Crossley tender
burst into the courtyard below, followed by twelve
motorcycle outriders and a Rolls Royce tourer.
The dapper, uniformed figure of Michael Collins
leapt from the car to the rostrum, saying:
'Judas Iscariot, I am arresting you for high treason
and for hijacking this Book. I wouldn't be
in your boots now, for you're sure to hang,
unless I'm mistaken.'
                              A haughty Judas scowled
defiance: 'Micky Collins, you won't pull this
one off. What makes you think Captain Flanagan
and the boys here won't just blow your brains out?'

Collins was either brave or barmy:
'Sure, they won't shoot me in my own country,' he said.

Time

Despite madness and heartache
Despite white supremacy and black magic
Despite heaven's rage and earthquake

Let's take a commercial break.

XI.   He will be mist

In They Swept

What I did for the politicians will never
Be properly evaluated.
Once the troubles were over, the miracles
Accomplished and acknowledged, the man dead,

Buried and resurrected as he said he'd be
To spectators at home in sin,
Terrified of grace in exile,
It was time for memory to be exploited
And politicians to move in.

And in they swept like a tide of leprosy
Like a plague of smile smile smile
Like an army of scabs to their own drill
Like a nightmare of handshakes
Like an unkillable smooth lie
Like me standing there, cold, looking up the hill.

The Old Style

I gave up treachery for Lent
And forced myself to meditate
On what sincerity meant.
I gazed long and long at the Irish Free State

Seeking a sincere man or woman.
Sincere. Sin seer. Won't do. I couldn't find
A single soul in the whole island
Whom I could, with all my heart and mind,

Dub sincere. But I tried, I tried, I really tried
Because I am a sticky lad
Once I get something into my head

But I failed, I failed, I really failed, and I sighed
Briefly before releasing the Judassmile
With 'I think I'll return to my old style.'

The Situation

In America when they want to know anything
About the situation, they ask him.
In England when they want to know anything
About the situation, they ask him.
He's the Great Authority, the Big Voice,
The High Mind in the know,
The Source that bright, bewildered men seek out
To find what's true

About the situation. And meanwhile I
Who brought the situation into being
Am left unquestioned in my chair, alone.

Why won't they ask me about the situation?
He's a slick articulate pig, I'm a king
Of fact and language, I'm the man, I cut to the bone,
I took part, I looked, I saw, I heard every word.
Why won't they ask me then? Why am I being ignored?
He's the Judas in the house, I'm the knowledgeable Lord.

Holding My Mirror Up to Nature *

I have a mirror in my room
Which now and then I look at
And am not surprised to see
A ferret or a rat
Terrorist or man of peace
Politician pauper diplomat
Jockey moneylender priest
Cornerboy knows where it's at.

One day I took this mirror out
Into streets of polluted light
And held it up to nature.

I swear the poison-clouded mirror laughed
A mocking scoffing chopping laugh.
I limped back home, conscious of diminished stature,

The structure
Of each distorted feature.

The Budding Pharmacist Broods On
The Second Biggest Problem In Ireland

'We had a two-day seminar on shit.
Professor Shaw
Speaking with his delicious Oxford wit
Said there was no discernable principle or law

Governing the ideal shit; yet he would say
That the conical-shaped, soft-textured plum
Replete with roughage and common in the
Fields and ditches of nineteenth-century Ireland

Was it.
Today, however, laxatives and purgatives
Are all the Irish can find.

It is the second biggest problem in the land.
Why, asked Profesor Shaw, do the Irish not realise
That shit is all in the mind?'

Flanagan's Crony

He drank his grief from a glass darkly.
It's a mercy he was taken quickly.

Christy Hannitty

Christy Hannitty was the most accomplished
Castrator of God's creatures in our pious island.
Ever since childhood, Christy wished
To perfect this most demanding craft.
        Bulls, pigs, rams, boys
And countless men victim-witnessed Christy's skill.
        If he could castrate women
Christy would've done that as well.
        Bloody hell!
He was known from Kerry to Donegal
For the gentle way he did the job,
Working his heart out, this most sensitive of souls.
He had one unwavering simple conviction
Which he enunciated with papalbull precision:
'I have all God's creatures by the balls.'

A Mystical Idea

Christy Hannitty thought it would be a blessing
If he cut the balls off all the Bishops of
Ireland because debollicked Bishops are less
Prone to the terrible temptations of love

Than those who are well-hung. Christy
Wrote a letter to Their Lordships, outlining
His plan for The New Purity Among Bishops.
Their Lordships read Hannitty's letter, noting

The crystal prose, the exact expression of a mystical
Idea, the juicy logic of the notion. They
Concluded, as a group, that they'd rather

Keep their balls intact, little as they used them.
They thanked Hannitty for his suggestion. Christy
Decided he'd take the matter up with the Holy Father.

A Stirring Account

Jesus took Christy Hannitty out for a meal
And wrote a stirring account of the event
In *Table for Two* in the *Squirish Mimes*:

      'The décor was Last Supperish, the waiters vaguely
Apostolic. I started with peasoup. Excellent.
Christy Hannitty had Dublin Bay prawns
Which looked radioactive to me but
Christy enjoyed them so I said nothing.
For the main course Christy had coddle.
I've rarely seen him look so contented.
I had colcannon. Succulent.
I changed some of the local water into wine
Pretty good though I got some dubious
Looks from the other customers. We finished off
With infinite cheeses, coffee, Napoleon Brandy, for a laugh.
The bill, which I paid hastily (Christy was inclined to pilfer
The spoons) came to thirty-one pieces of silver.
Strolling home, Christy sang *Roll Me Over in the Clover*.'

Hot

Don't tell me the world isn't ruled by liars
Like me. Schultz put all the rebels to rout,
Organised a dinner for the sellers and buyers
Of truth because truth, says Schultz, will out.

Pilate, recently, in a petit bourgeois setting,
Phantomed among sheets and shirts flapping about his head;
Schultz, passing, asked Pilate what he was getting
Up to. 'Hanging out my dirty washing' Pilate said.

By all means let us have a Last Judgment.
Let bank clerks and shopkeepers comprise the jury,
Let the sharpest minds analyse this cosmic rot

While for the umpteenth time the veil of the temple is rent
And I, neat as a flea, fresh as a berry,
Coax the whore truth to bed and fuck her while she's hot.

With Such Passion

The Church bugged the room where the Last
Supper was held because it wanted to know
Down to the final detail, exactly what the most
Wanted men in that part of the world were up to

On that particular evening. As the night wore on
The apostles grew more and more tipsy,
Tongues loosened, old rivalries flared in
The usual way and it fell to Christ
To keep the men in a tolerably harmonious
State. He talked about bread and wine, body
And blood. He asked to be remembered in like fashion.

The Church was listening to all this
But couldn't quite grasp it. 'Has the wine gone to
Jesus's head' muttered The Church, 'that he should speak with
        such passion?'

A Pitiless Scrubbing

My knowledge of politicians is limited
To the private but passionate conviction
They're more attractive dead than alive.
One politician informs me he thinks
Pontius Pilate a fascinating figure
Capable of governing many lands.
My own experience of the Roman suggests
He's rather too fond of washing his hands.

Winter and summer, by day and night,
Before, during, after drinking and eating,
Following peaceful strolls through green

Unpolluted countryside, Pilate can't wait
To give his hands a pitiless scrubbing.
You'd swear he believes they'll never be clean.

Crutch *

My fascist friends are insanely clean.
I've never found anything even remotely filthy
In what is called pornographic and obscene.
The real thing is spotless, never heard of dirty,

I've searched high and low
For even a faint stain, a single scruffy spot
But no go, no go.
Dirty it is not.

My encounters with clean evil are such
I am determined now
To be a dirty old man.

Well, everyone, or nearly everyone, needs a crutch.
I will go low, low, lower than I've ever been
To see how it all began,
To see, touch, sniff that original stain.

Meaning *

Murmur the name over and over:
You'll know the meaning of enemy, lover.

A Motion

I decided The Church's name should be changed
To the Losers' Club. I put the motion to The Church.
'Why?' queried The Church.

        'You've become unhinged
With caution' I replied, 'You've lost the sense of search –
You're out of touch with your origin, the man
Who died for me, you wear pompous clothes,
You eat too much, you're too fond of money,
When did you last smell the Mystical Rose?
Everything you do smacks of vanity and defeat,
You take heaven for granted,
You need to get back in the gutter, you need
To bleed profusely for a while,
You need to dynamise your style, you need to admit
You're the Losers' Club before you're new again.'

'Motion rejected' smiled The Church, 'Let us now pass on.'

Purified

Pretend to be what they believe you are
You are what they believe they think
They want a guiding star you are that star
Want hope, be hope, exist to rise and sink

And listen to the wind that knocks the house.
They want a victim, grab the victim-role
They need a traitor then be treacherous
And feel damnation amplify your soul

They're nothing
But won't allow you to be nothing too.
You must be someone, that's your fate.

Walk where the cliffs are crumbling
Towards the sea so murderously blue
It looks like eyes eyes eyes purified by hate.

The Line

Here's the line, he said,
Cross it, you're a goner.

I looked at the line:
Straight, black, absolutely there.

Stay at your side of the line, he said,
Or it's curtains for you, chum.

Why, I asked, did you draw the line
Down the middle of the bed
Since the bed is big enough to contain
Without bother to either, two grown men?

I sleep this side, he said,
You sleep that side. Right?

Right, I replied, I swear
I'll never cross the line.

If, however, he said, my leg strays across
The line, you'll understand, won't you?

That'd be an accident, I said,
How could I blame you for that?

Thanks, he sighed, I feel better now,
Knowing I won't be punished if I go astray.

Sweet and deep be your sleep, I murmured,
The line is there between us to keep us together.

You have a way with words, he said,
And dozed off. So did I, the straight
Black absolute line down the middle of the bed,
Down the middle of my head.

A Modest Advertising Campaign

You would think, would you not, that it would be
A most difficult task
To get people to purchase my Pure Poisons
Manufactured in my personal factory
In Listowel. In fact, all I had to do
Was mount a modest advertising campaign
Stressing the value of Judaspoison to all who
Are interested in the true nature of man.

Within three days, my poisons found their way
Into the mouths of lawyers teachers priests
Doctors executives entertainers clowns bores
News announcers continuity girls actors poets
Shopkeepers publicans professors editors bishops
And the busy cunts of profiteering whores.

You Bright Young Things *

After my suicide picture appeared on TV –
        Stylishly I dangled, bearded and pop-eyed
        From the dependable tree –
There followed a spate of copycat suicides

        Among people of all classes.
Are these folk, I ask myself, a pathetic shower
        Of simple-minded asses
Lacking even a modicum of power
To resist the example of a job well-done
        Or are they secretly in sympathy with what
                I struggled to achieve
And manifestly did not?

Or did I? How shall I ever know?
Speak up, you bright young things in the front row,
You information maniacs, you mesmerized gazers at screens,
You who will never become pathetic hasbeens.

Impossible

Conspiracy is impossible to disprove.
Am I involved in one? Are you?
If you are, are not, how do you know?
I/you go about our work, eat
Sandwiches at breaks, face every task,
Draw the pay, pay the tax, enjoy
The weekends, endure Mondays and never ask
Is this a conspiracy?

Can I prove it's not?
Will you insist it is?
Victims? Perpetrators? Or someone not like
Either? Do we love the rut?
Break it, have we friends who'll write
To the papers if we go on hunger-strike?
Start a 'Free Judas' campaign
When prison-doctors find
I'm going blind?

Blind. I'll never see you again
And all I see in my starving dark
Is open to question.
Question me under a blinding light.
Ring me with lie-detectors, skilled perjurors.
I'm a hopelessly ignorant man.
I have no answers, none.

XII. The True Thing

I've Only So Much Blood

Dear me, to have reached such heights, such depths,
And then to find a mosquito
Has the upper hand in the hot, foreign night.
Cute little bloodsucker, specialist in vertigo,
Dive-bomber close to my ear,
Such a mighty whine from such a little thing
Creating one more tiny civilised fear.
I've only so much blood. Therefore I sing
Of languages I cannot learn
Dream-images I'll never understand
Neighbours I never dare to know
Delusions of logic among philosophers
This notion I have of living where a few
Decent moments flourish and grow.

Taste

To savour the full taste of betrayal
One must half-love one's victim
And be wholly loved by him
Or her or it or they or all together in a shining choir

Such as, old voices say, surrounds the heavenly throne
In eternal perfection. I take a lamb,
A sheep, a cat, a man, a dog, I call the thing my own,
I savour nature, I betray therefore I am.

Language is a farce.
The fascist flesh rules you and me.
No words can shape the curse.
I lock my lips on nothing and go free

To mope at street-corners
Give pet-names to stars
Ruminate on the factors
That influence the blood of traitors.

Field Day

I once tried by hook and by crook
To collect the scattered thoughts
Of the Apostles and their apostles
And publish them in one helluva book.
It was a massive task involving
Research among thieves robbers hitmen whores,
Disentangling strands of public rhetoric
Barbed whispers behind closed doors.

Let me say this: I had a field day
Digging up these thoughts from everywhere
Writing them down, knocking them into shape.

My book says what I've heard people say
At guarded and unguarded moments here
And there. Get it. Read it. There's no escape.

Parodies

The more real the man is the more intent
The pigs are on reducing him
To a crucified parody of himself.
Terror of the real deepens their cry for killing.

I have an unparodied beat in my blood, whether
Good or bad, well I'll leave that up to yourself.
But don't forget, we're in the crucifying business together.

Where I come from is nailed with old stories
Like a field studded with thorns and stones.
We heap mockery on skeletons.
I heard a yarn today grinning through a circle of men:
'Down Baggot Street I saw a tinker's pony
Cartin' a load o' dung. "See!" I said, "Paddy Kavanagh
Is lookin' for digs. The fuckin' poet is homeless again!"'

The lads broke their arses laughin'.

A Chanting Ring

The words, sick of folk like you and me,
Escaped, hid under seaweed,
Green weed bloodblackening in decay.
If birds gulped this, they'd die.
Should fish flounder here, they'd gape
Like snotty poets who can't take their drink.
If ailing women crutched here, they'd melt
And spread their sickness like the ways we think.
And who's this man of the horse and cart
Gathering weed now the sea is away
Balancing the world, giving the other side a chance?

He packs the weed into the cart, drives
Over the sand where the sea will be
And not be, and be again, like missionaries
Working on children in a chanting ring,
Acolytes glowing near gods who teach them how to sing
Of matters happy beyond all understanding.

Once, somewhere

Language hides its face in shame and is no longer willing
To speak of earth or hell or heaven
Or the bloodmarvel of ordinary feeling.
'Look at the lovely picture the child made out of nothing.'

It's a beautiful morning for a killing,
The patriots have struck again, it takes seven
To murder a man, and now they're cheering
Down the lane where he walked as a boy,
As a man with the extraordinary intention of
Working in hopes of settling with his girl
And fathering children to grow in love.
Love! Jeers flood river and lake
Cheers ripridicule the countryside
The sun pukes mockery on roads fields hills
His girl begins to break
The patriots have found a place where language cannot live
The hills are splitting into lunatic screams
The child's lovely pictures are obscene dreams
There is no word that is not a bad mistake.
        Someone prayed once, somewhere, o for God's sake
Don't make me laugh, I could die laughing
At words twisting in their pain,
Murder cheering down the lane.

A Broken Back *

I saw the rhythm breaking its back
On the riverbank close to the musical wood.
The crack of the breaking back sent a shock
Through every known and unknown solitude
        So that I hungered to see
If there was anything I could do for the
        Broken-backed rhythm
Lying there with agonised eyes
Dumb-incredulous
After fluent centuries.

        I wanted to fling question after question
At the stricken rhythm. I wanted to know
        If it felt betrayed,
If it thought it might recover in time
Or if all sense of itself would vanish now that its back
        Was broken.
        Instead I stayed silent

As when, in the presence of the dead, I turn
   Over and over in my mind

The familiar, mysterious name
Drifting farther and farther beyond my comprehension
Until infinite bewildering distance is my own helpless
   Repetition.

A Winner

Outside the Bank of Ireland she stood
And gazed up at the statue of Grattan.
'Excuse me, sir' she said, 'Don't think me odd
If I read you a poem from the Latin.

Though it was written quite some time ago
These lines will touch your stony heart
For in your day you could be moved, I know,
By choice specimens of the poetic art.

The poem concerns a lady who must choose
Between putting her tongue in this chap's mouth
Or up his arse. She chose his arse. 'Twas cleaner.'

So saying, she read the Latin poem. My views
On poetry are amateur. It has to do with truth,
I hear. Grattan froze. I smiled. The lady picked a winner.
The Bank of Ireland glowed like a belly after dinner.

Judges *

I, too, have heard the voices of gravestones,
Incorruptible judges of old, wily skeletons.
Stripped of everything but the wisdom of bones.

Bad Language

'One fine day, a scrupulous anti-pollutionist
Dumped all the poets in a river,'
The playwright said.
                         'The river was deep
Enough to swallow each self-scratching creep,
The poets began to gasp, splutter, flounder
Like flies in melted butter, they
Started to sink, it was sad, I was tempted to weep
Because here, drowning before my eyes
Were the spouters of all that's true beautiful wise,
All the creators of beauty in my time.
I stood on the bank, gazing, feeling my soul
Rapt-tragic. Suddenly I saw a log come

From nowhere like a poem, the poets saw it too, they began
To grab the log but there were too many drowning
Bards whacking and strangling each other like madmen
In a black parody of inspiration,
They sank in their own clatter, groaning curses
Such as you might find enshrined in satanic verses.

I have never seen so many poets sinking together
Amid such bad language, in such chaste weather.
That mass-drowning shrieks in me. May I never spectate another.'

Original Manuscripts

'I ran into Paddy Kavanagh one mornin'
And asked him how he felt.
"Fuckin' awful," he replied, "I'm kilt shakin',
Half-blind, bloody bored, in terrible health
'Cos I was up all night writin'
The Great Fuckin' Hunger
For a Famous Institution
Interested in buyin' original manuscripts.
Sure I often claned me arse with poems
Not realisin' I was wipin' shite with cash.

I'll wangle money outa these bastards:
They think they're buyin' me fuckin' classic."

Course we all know his poems sing like a bird.
Isn't that the gassest yarn yez ever fuckin' heard?'

Baptism

Three businessmen, roused, threw the poet
Kavanagh into the Grand Canal
In Dublin. Enraged by hit after hit
Of his venomous persisting wit,
Animated by his ridicule,
They drowned him one misty November night.

      Down in the accommodating waters
Kavanagh called on his won't-take-no-for-an-answer God
      Who was pleased to display His might.
He plucked the poet from the murderous cold.

Kavanagh got the loan of a suit from a friend
In a merciful flat in Pembroke Road.
      Spick and span
      This poetman
Returned to the pub where the businessmen
Celebrated the drowning of the gadfly.
They gulped at the ghost who ordered a large whiskey
And said 'Thanks for the baptism, lads. I'm born again.'

Send a Letter

Out of the awful silence of the God of nothing
A voice, then voices: 'Of course, you pig,
You dare not know it,
Judas is the ultimate poet.'
I'd heard that vilest of bad rhymes
Before, in a sacrificial slum,

But now...ultimate? H'mm.
                    I'd never dreamed
There's nothing as treacherous as poetry
(Musical expression of the total man)
Not even the poet. Fly lads! Fly lassies!
Who suffered for this? Not the concern of these
Fly-by-night lines sparking a damned head
Convinced the sense of waste ends only when you're dead
And morning coughs in like a sub-editor
With a style like a leaking coffin,
Flush with an apt quotation
From *The Third Coming*,
Tubercular with the notion
That something important is being said.
Nothing I've ever read, said, heard said
Deserves to be remembered.
Another amateur Judas achieves a catharsis.
Say it. They'll gulp it. People are customers.
Old customers die hard. Say it. You'll feel better.
Who suffered for this? If you know, send a letter.

Again

Language Pathology, scrupulously pursued
By erudite women and men,
Is likely to come to a sticky end
Unless the word becomes flesh again

And not the flesh of sheep or cows
Or horses past their prime
To be scoffed in eating-places and watering-holes
By the plushest bellies of our time

But the flesh of the words of condemned men
Waiting on Death Row
For an end to the farce

Or the words of a whore in Merrion Square
Whose reputation as an AIDS-carrier has no
Visible effect on her eloquent arse.

The Present Writer

I saw the present writer stretched face
Down on the floor of a mucky place
In a posture of moan-and-groan disgrace.
      I studied him.

His face was unctioned in the muck
Like a speculator's mind in the Stock Exchange.
I couldn't see his eyes, they drowned beyond my range,
A feasting creature squatted on his neck.

His fingers flicked like rats among the filth
His odour caused the world to block its nose
There was some blood but no, the genius was not gory.

Others fled, I approached and said, 'Your health
Is vile, your vision slanted, your style uncommon. Rise
Up, you stinking get, and tell my story.'

As from the dead, he upped. The rest is commentary.

A Voice at Last

I had this fierce impulse to be a spokesman once.
I looked around for a cause: the poor, the sick,
The inexplicably shivering, the blacks, the Irish, the AIDS
Lot, starving millions, alcos, the blind, the dumb,
Tinkers, illiterates, the homeless, the Rock
Of Gibraltar victims, occupants of our choice jails,
Battered wives, battered husbands, battered pig-castrators.
All these sprang to mind, to nose, to eye.
Should I speak for them? No, I thought not,
They had their spokesmen and women, I pondered, I
Suddenly decided to be the first spokesman for

Nothing, I studied it in my breast, in yours,
In all the victims I have mentioned elsewhere,
I spoke out, nobody listened, everyone
Thought he was something, I persisted,

Slowly, the scene changed, my best endeavours
Tell me that nothing is coming into its own,
Nothing has a voice at last. Listen! Listen!

Ah, wrong again, Judas, old skin!
Jesus, why am I always getting it wrong?
Why can't I just up and say
It is not the voice of nothing
I wish to hear, to let speak
Over the valium towns and crammed
Cities, but the perfectly human
Voice of the fleshy damned?
And to what, my soul-mates, are we damned?
Nothing spectacular, I assure you, nothing
To excite emetic revulsion or epic shock;
Only, at certain moments, the sight and smell
Of accumulated shite
On a babbling Atlantic rock.

Revelations

It is true I fail at the level of language
When I try to translate the various parts
Of myself into words to be read by others
Interested in verbal revelations of the heart.

My gizzard, for example, my colon, my lights
Functioning in my body's darkness
Remind me of those nomad desert tribes
Moving through silence out of silence into silence.

Are they escaping a doom? Or embracing one?

Consider my brain ticking like a nailbomb
In a bag outside a supermarket
Winning the present phase of the prices war.
Who'll be passing when the nailbomb kicks?

There's the odorous slot in my bum,
My veins bearing the sign 'Rare blood to let'
And my lips, my God, what shall I say of my lips?

The Years Are Words

Being your own hangman demands
A poetic sense of timing.
In that final stanza you discover
Sweet secrets of rhythm and rhyming.
While the blood speaks in your ears
A true blessing, a true curse,
The logic of your life is clear
As the argument of verse.
Dancing spots before your eyes
Are metaphors on a spree,
Your true music is heard at last,
The years are words grown bright and wise,
Lucid, right, ecstatically free.
So hang yourself and celebrate your past.

A Hot Knife

A man is writing a poem about me
Raping paper with me in his head
Thinking he knows something about treachery
And anarchy blackening my blood.
Can he tell loneliness from solitude?
Does he know what I believe and cannot believe?
Does his notion of God touch my notion of God?
What has he lived of love?
                        I'm tickled to death
By people who think they know
Shallows and depths of somebody else.
                        I have such a pain today,
A hot knife in my wrist, my back, my head,
My heart, my eyes, my unpredictable pulse,
I think I'll hide somewhere and sweat away my pain.
If that man finds it, it'll chutzpah his poem.

W.H. Goes Walking

Of course it's you, in optimistic mood,
A Hellenised Jew from Alexandria
Visiting an intellectual friend.
You're walking together, your way takes you

Past the base of Golgotha. Looking up
You see an all too familiar sight –
Three crosses surrounded by a jeering crowd.
Frowning in distaste, you say 'It's disgusting

How the mob enjoys this sort of thing.
Why can't the authorities execute criminals
Humanely, in private, put hemlock in their blood

Like Socrates?' You're upset. Then, averting
Your eyes from this vile spectacle,
You resume your discussion of the True, the Beautiful, the Good.

Spiritflowers

I decided at an early age that everything
I touched would be artistic.
I would teach my demons how to sing
I would transform all my sick
Moments into poems of my spirit
Seducing the petty mind and shrunken soul
Out of their natural inclination towards rot
Into spiritflowers flourishing in full

Glory. I planned to take my mean heart,
Make it a magnanimous work of art
Where every spat-on outcast might belong
And even old injustice feel at home.
This dream I had of myself. My dream said 'Come.'
But I could not. Why? God knows. Something went wrong.
Who knows what horrors go to make a song?

I Understand *

Whatever about others, it is vital to have no
Mercy on oneself.
                    That's the shape
My thought took
                    as I witnessed the snow
Telling white lies to my favourite landscape,
Transfiguring it as though
It were a bride
                    on a crisp March morning.
O God of Heaven, Jerusalem and the Gap of Dunloe

Listen to her laughing!

As her laughter transfigures the world
I understand the love-belief that says
All men are brothers

And I understand
Why I must never have mercy on myself
Whatever about others.

Milk

One morning in my bedsit, being visionary,
I began to paint a picture –
Baby Jesus at the bare breast of Mary,
God drinking milk from his mother.
I have never seen a more beautiful breast
Nor has there ever been a more sustaining milk,
Creation thrilled me, blood in my fingers,
Heaven warming my heart, I was blessed,
I know I was blessed but hell appeared, millions of devils
Opened their mouths, black teeth unwashed since God knows when,
Throats howling 'Mary, we thirst! Please! Please!'
Mary looks down, takes her breast from Jesus's mouth,
Squirts milk on the devils, they drink like hell,
I like the picture, it's called *A Moment of Ease*.

Thread *

Within minutes of each other
That November morning
I saw a shooting star
And a shrivelled leaf
In the shape of a claw.

And I saw my tiny self
Become a thread between leaf and star
On which were strung like pearls
The souls of my dead
Father mother friends.

Was I remembering
Or were they singing
Of one living
As best he can,
Fiery, withering man?
Quick, visioning man?
Ageless, treacherous man?

My Simple Wish *

I am trying not to be known but you'll insist
On fingering me as the man
Responsible for the stranger's crucifixion
On the hill of bloodlust.
Well, it had to be someone, hadn't it?
If I hadn't done it, would you now own
That cosy pad in the shadow of the Cathedral
Strangers gaze at in admiration?

Despite this atrocity
All I want to do is retire to a lakeside cottage
Where people will accept me and leave me alone.

I shall raise bees, develop curative honey
That may help to lessen your primitive rage
At my simple wish to be completely unknown.

Reader's Report

At first I thought this a typical New Realism job
But I warmed to the writing as I read on.
A great deal hangs on the portrayal of the central character,
His pained involvement with the world about him,
His attitudes to women including his mother
His deft way with miracles, concise use
Of imagery in those punchy little parables
And his complex relationships with Romans and Jews.

Supporting characters are, on the whole, credibly drawn,
The style simple but effective, the plot
Swings through various worlds, heavens and hells.

That grisly scene on the hill verges on
Melodrama but the aftermath has a joyous
Magic. I recommend a large paperback edition.
I'll bet it sells.

What's That?

What is God but ourselves
Hearing in eternity
The voices of those we loved
In the poor opportunity of time?

                    Not a bad start
But there I go again, never able to finish anything,
Betraying the promise, the beginning.

                This morning's quizzical clouds are works of art
Flung out as carelessly as the salutations
Of schoolkids to each other but here I sit
Turning the key in the lock
Of my heart. In there, maybe, I'll be able to listen,
I may even dare to finish what I set out
To say. What's that? Tell me or by Jesus I'll go on strike.

I Read a Poem Once

Those who believe they deal in revelation
Are sometimes traitors.
When I see their attempts to give body to vision
I recognise my brothers
Rehearsing in lyrical terms that death-rattle
Characteristic of emotional has-beens.
I am touched, or almost touched, by their prattle
Of integrity, whatever that means.

Therefore, my brothers, embrace a cause.
Champion the fascist or revolutionary dance,
Herod, Judas, Hitler, your bittersweet affair with God.
Suffer the chaos but observe the laws.
Be sullen and poetic, complain, I read a poem once,
Incoherent stuff, written in blood.
How can bad eyes recognise the good?

There, If Anywhere

A rough man began to shout near the temple,
'Woe to the city! Woe to the nation!'
Day and night he bellowed warning to the streets.
Roused by his noising, prominent citizens
Grabbed and beat him. He would not apologise
Or accuse his attackers. Mere fear he did not show.
The district magistrate ordered he be flogged;
Later, judging him mad, let him go.

The rough man continued like this, seven years.
One day, walking under the walls, he shouted
'Woe to the city! Woe to the nation!' Then, 'Woe is me!'
A stone, fired from somewhere like nowhere,
Hit him and killed him. He bellowed
No more woe. Where did I hear that story?
Why am I owned by this clumsy art?

If there's a way to fight the nothing in the heart
It must be a story. O I have mine but when
I try to tell it to a man or woman
It's all bits and pieces
Like walking by the shore alone
Some winter morning when the tide is out.
I have a plastic bag to put my story in:
Bits of driftwood first, polished by my favourite
Sculptor, the sea. Here's a dead widgeon
To hang around my neck;
Here's a stab of green glass smooth and wicked
As a persuading tongue;
Here's a terrier pup drowned near a rock,
Frozen hard as the sense of wrong.
My bits and pieces accumulate; the story makes itself;
There, if anywhere, I am trapped enough to belong.

Hellhot Cakes

It takes a solitary scholar like me, not a tribal
Dabbler like Hitler to translate
The tricky Termonfecken Bible
From the Hebrew Irish Greek and Aramaic.

All through the work it was my wish
To eschew the gross familiarities of slang
For undefiled and dignified English.
My footnotes, thick with scholarship, rang

True. All indelicacies I brushed aside.
My Jesuit advisers suggested I
Review the book myself, taking whatever line

Seemed wisest. I prayed I cried I prayed.
And then 'Fuck it' I said 'I'll give the thing a try.'
My review was critical but benign.

The Professor of Bibles at Oxford
Objected on the grounds
I should not write about my own production.

He made pedantic sounds.
My version failed, he said, at the level of language.
'Fear not, it is I' Christ said
When he went for a walk on the water.
My translation ran 'I'm in deep, above my head.'

I wonder if people understand
Water-walking is advanced aquatic art
Perfectible only after millions of mistakes.

Even then a man might sink at any time.
I told the Professor of Bibles to go fart.
My paperback is selling like hellhot cakes.

Satisfied

During a recent pilgrimage to hell
I was entertained by the spectacle
Of one poet eating another.
Some poets eat devilishly well.

Poet number one knifed poet number two,
Sliced and nibbled his left testicle
Then cut the tongue, a cool parnassian blue,
Chewed, savoured, pronounced it delectable.

Poet number two emitted epic cries
Knowing his paradise was lost.
Poet number one looked at him askance,
Tried some brain, sipped some blood, guzzled the eyes
And then, satisfied (I thought) at last,
Performed a dandy iambic dance.

The Point

Now let me see...

A man I distrust frequently begins his sentences
'The truth is, of course.'
His grin confirms possession of the truth
While you are a floundering barbarian, or worse,
Some garrulous nitwit infected with enthusiasm
Of the more unfortunate kind. So shut up, you.
He goes on to reveal the essence of everything
While you melt with respect in the presence of the true.

Living in the sweet grip of revelation
May be a challenge for some, but not him
Quietly content with total vision,
Tolerant, also, of the blind and dumb
Surrounding him, although among the dumb and blind
Lie truthful titbits he may never find.
The same gentleman is fit to wet his pants
If, in listening to your talk or reading what you write,
He cannot quickly see 'the point'.
Ah! The Point!

> *I read a poem last week*
> *   And I couldn't see the point!*
> *I heard a song last night*
> *   And I couldn't see the point!*
> *I looked at all these prisoners' paintings*
> *   And for the life of me – no point!*
> *I read that Northern woman on how we live down here –*
> *   What on earth is the woman's point?*

May one man kiss
Another and enjoy his own snake's hiss?
Blood on your white bread?
Steely creatures chewing the insides of your head?
My youngest brother with a petrol
Bomb in one hand and a stone in the other?
O days when times and crimes are out of joint
The point is your damned terror of the point
Whatever that may be.
Now let me see...

All the Terrified Strangers

Anything but this!

                      I peel away the bandage
To reveal the wound, I peel away the skin
To show the flesh, I strip the flesh,
                            the bone
Blushes at my touch, I see a face then,
The eyes cry for all the terrified strangers
Living in me, in you, me, you, men, men.
I love you. No, screams the bone, never say these
Words again.

Humanpoem

I have tried to die but you won't let me.
I went to the hell of a lot of trouble
To end my experiment in misery.
This was no off-the-cuff arrangement,
No sudden twist at the top of the stairs,
Dart into the bathroom and Bob's your uncle
Behind the door; nor was it a slow
Mangy erosion of my personality
Culminating in farcical vertigo
And an irrefutable affirmation
Of that much talked-about ultimate erection.

This was, like all I did, a work of art,
A sculptured commitment to the notion of oblivion,
A humanpoem, flower of a human seed
There in the open air for any traveller to read
And interpret according to his need.
Physicians of my youth, darlings of my first thrust,
Victims and witnesses of my not innocuous lust,
Chief influences of my contemplative brow,
Where are you now?

For I have failed to put an end to what
Has constantly disgusted me, the thought
Of myself. Here I go
Lurching down Bride Street with a reeking
Drunk, listening to an over-taxed teacher
Railing against the hooligans he pretends to educate
('There's one cunt I'd crucify on any wooden gate');
And if I risk paper, television or radio,
These political voices I adore-abhor, I heard them
In better weather two thousand years ago
Or more. It is for these
Recurring delicacies you keep alive
This eternal judasflower, humanpoem. You are my
Nourisher.
Am I the answer to your prayer?

A Beautiful Mind

Recently I met
One of the unacknowledged legislators of mankind.
He struck me as being a bit of a wet
Though he had a beautiful mind.

He loved everything, especially himself.
His voice souped out of a dream.
He fidgeted. 'What's wrong?' I asked.
He said 'I can't find a theme.'

Now if there's one creature who moves me to the core
It's an unacknowledged, themeless legislator.
That's a hard double-burden for a singer to bear.
I was so moved I could endure no more.
'Take me as a theme' I offered, 'Dig! Explore!'
'No!' snarled the bard 'You're bad news for my Muse.
Vamoose! Piss off! Scram out of here!'

As I gazed on the trembling spirit standing there
Sensitive behind his beard like a poetic God The Father
I mused on the power of poetry
To capture bright sparks of eternity
And I mused also on how little
Love and hope there is in our world,
Certain parts of which persist in some distress,
And I thought how poets wage a spiritual battle
To shed some light on the unprofitable mess,
Blessing what others curse, cursing what others bless.
I wanted to utter my thoughts to the nervous
Representative of that sublime art, themeless before me,
But I held my tongue.

Instead I offered him a cup of Eden applejuice
With which to quench his Parnassian thirst
And refresh him into song.

He drank the juice. Now I must wait to find
What flowers startle from that beautiful mind.
And wait I will, for I'm a patient lad
Willing to sniff all flowers, good and bad.

One *

If I can rub the world out of my eyes
God knows what I'll see this morning.
I know a thousand ways to be blind
And one of seeing.

I Have My Doubts

Suppose there's nothing that is not a sad mistake.
Suppose my own version of the Good Book
In which I play a part of tragical bad luck
Though promising at the start, is but a fake.

Suppose all the talk of truth is a bag of lies
Like ripening tumours in an honest brain.
Suppose love with its sweet agonies and sighs
Is a gadding cancer through available veins.

Suppose dear god's a devil with a sense of fun
– who's reading this? –
And wrote the script for us, his natural actors,
To play the parts until the play is done.
It never is. My mind is melancholy because
I have my doubts. And there are other factors.

Play

I once tried my hand at an old-fashioned morality play.
Following long haggling with the management
The thing was performed at the Gabby Theatre.
The play was called *Whoever Said I Can't*.

The three principal parts were myself, Jesus and God.
I played the part of Jesus and he, me.
God played himself and was a howling success.
Some of the audience got riled because they couldn't see him.

I found it hard to get into the part of Jesus.
The heart of his matter was somehow beyond me
And my delivery of his parables lacked passion.
He, on the other hand, was a startling Judas
As though he knew my soul so completely
Every word gesture silence revealed me as touchingly human.
He brought me into the light
From the darkness of a thousand graves.
The play was vigorously reviewed, several raves:
'Jesus a revelation as Judas'
'Judas captivatingly ambiguous as Jesus'
'God impresses with his invisibility'.

After long runs in Dublin and London
We decided to tour the Irish provinces
Encouraged by a fat grant from the Arts Council.
In towns of Ulster Leinster Munster Connaught
Whoever Says I Can't proved that it could
Touch the hearts and souls of the common people.
Their nightly applause was passionate and long.
'D'you think they know what's happening?' I asked God.

'They think they do, and that's what matters' he replied with a smile,
'Great actors will make people believe anything
They choose
From Peace In Our Time to the Conversion of the Jews.'

I was pleased, but didn't let it go to my head,
Happy that simple, old-fashioned morality was not entirely dead.

The True Thing

I don't know anyone who knows what became of the true thing.
If poets think they sing, it is a parody they sing.
In the beginning men of common sense
Knew that for the damned dream to grow
Wholesale massacre of innocence
Was necessary, prophets' blood must flow,
Thieves of little apples be crucified, rebels be put down,
Conspiracies of messianic troglodytes be strangled
And saviours be given the bum's rush out of every pub in town.

Out of the smashed cities
Works of art adorn the Vatican walls
A comfortable living is right for the Archbishop and his wife
Lads and lassies study till their eyeballs burn and their souls know
One must never heed the bitter cries, forsaken calls
Of the man in the beginning burning fear
Like old papers, kissing his death, having given his life.
Yes, and we have double-glazed hearts and committees and
            promotions and pensions

And time off to enjoy and bless
The kids shining out to discos and parties
In the holy light of progress.
And we have learning, we could put Hell in a couplet, Eden in an
      epigram,
Dish out slices of epics like gifts of land in the Golden Vale
And sweat blood or what feels like blood
To get the right rhythm and thereby hangs a tale
Of an abortive experiment in love
That began in bestial company and ended in public shame
And started all over again in a sad parody
Of what cannot be understood

Only followed as a blind man follows his expensive dog
Through visionary streets of fluent slavish traffic
Calmly-crazily living the rhythms of my mechanical blood
Yearning occasionally, nevertheless, for dialogue with God.
I would ask, to begin with, what became of the true thing
And after that, well, anything might happen.
I can even imagine a poet starting to sing
In a way I haven't heard for a long time.
If the song comes right, the true thing may find a name
Singing to me of who, and why, I am.

All Over Again *

You know how, as a man shrivels older,
He dreams of returning to certain places
He knew when he was young.
The world is a womb.

I'm two thousand years old.

Every few hundred years, I go back
To the room where we had the Last Supper,
I sit at the table, in my ageless position,
I sip a glass of wine, I see
Happy, celebrating men.

He looks at me.

It happens all over again.
It's like living a poem that whips me
Back and forth and in and out of time
Until I almost know what it means to be human.

A fearless man
Wants to change this rotten place,
I hear him speak, I see
Love and courage light his face.
He chooses followers, I want to be
A follower, I want to change
The rotten scene, I know
What causes men to rot.
This knowledge concentrates my thought.

I want to talk about it, man to man.
I want to work with him.

But first, let's analyse everything.
Let's commandeer the energy
Of the chosen few.
Let's get the incentives right.
Let's call a special meeting.

We need a strategic plan.

And yes, of course, I'll do everything I can
To look after the money.

I'm your man.

Let the myths begin.